Putting Family First

Putting Family First

Successful Strategies
for Reclaiming Family Life
in a Hurry-Up World

❈

William J. Doherty, Ph.D.,
and Barbara Z. Carlson

An Owl Book
Henry Holt and Company • New York

Henry Holt and Company, LLC
Publishers since 1866
115 West 18th Street
New York, New York 10011

Henry Holt® is a registered trademark
of Henry Holt and Company, LLC.

Portions of chapters 8–11 are adapted from William Doherty's books
The Intentional Family (Avon, 1997), *Take Back Your Kids* (Sorin, 2000),
and *Take Back Your Marriage* (Guilford, 2001).

The story "Finding Willoughby" by Bugs Peterschmidt is reprinted
by permission of *Guideposts* magazine.

Library of Congress Cataloging-in-Publication Data
Doherty, William J. (William Joseph), date.
  Putting family first : successful strategies for reclaiming
family life in a hurry-up world / William J. Doherty
and Barbara Z. Carlson.
    p. cm.
  Includes index.
  ISBN 0-8050-6838-4 (pbk.)
    1. Family—United States.   2. Family—Time management—
United States.   3. Parenting—United States.   I. Carlson, Barbara Z.
II. Title.

HQ536 .D644   2002
306.85'0973—dc21   2002017237

Henry Holt books are available for special promotions and
premiums. For details contact: Director, Special Markets.

First Edition 2002
Designed by Victoria Hartman
Printed in the United States of America

1   3   5   7   9   10   8   6   4   2

With love we dedicate this book
to those who make us family:
Leah, Eric, Elizabeth Doherty,
Sam, Adam, Britt, Laura, Joshua Carlson,
Angela and Matthew LaJoy

Contents

Introduction

We finished writing the body of this book on the morning of September 11, 2001, a tragic day seared into the consciousness of all Americans. Two weeks later, we write this introduction in a nation reeling from loss, its boundaries violently breached and its sense of invulnerability shattered. After the disaster occurred, we momentarily wondered whether anyone would care about the theme of this book—how to reclaim family life from frantic schedules. The answer came these past two weeks from our fellow citizens, whose actions testified boldly to the importance of families.

When hijacked airline passengers found telephones, they called their spouses or parents to say "I love you" and "good-bye."

When office workers in the World Trade Center felt the shock of the airplane collisions and saw the smoke, they called a family member to offer reassurance that they would get out safely.

When the rest of us heard the news of the attacks, we first called our spouses, children, parents, or siblings.

Parents everywhere gathered their children around them. Some went to their children's schools that day to bring them home. Some scoured the news media for ideas about how to talk to their children about these horrific events. Others worried about their sons being sent to war.

Many of us thought of deceased family members during these days. Bill experienced feelings of relief that his father, who cared deeply for this country and who had lived through the Great Depression, Pearl Harbor, and World War II, was not alive to witness this tragedy. Bill was surprised to hear from friends who had the same feelings about deceased parents from a generation who had paid their dues and were now spared this new, confusing, and long-term struggle.

As the mother of two sons, Barbara was immediately gripped with thoughts of her mother and grandmother and how they must have felt sending off an eighteen-year-old brother and son to war. How did they ever deal with the news two years later that this boy would never come home?

We know that not all families are connected enough to be helpful in such a crisis. A mental health worker in New York recounted that the most distressed survivors he encountered during the immediate aftermath of the attacks were people who were cut off from family members and uncertain if they could call them for support.

The message could not be clearer: family relationships are the irreplaceable core of a full human life. It sometimes takes a personal or national tragedy to remind us of this simple truth—that family life is first. A rich family life alone is not enough, of course, because we also need strong neighborhoods, schools, communities of values and beliefs, governments, nations, and a cooperative international community. But none of these, alone or together, can substitute for family life.

We wrote this book for two reasons: because we are alarmed about how the frantic pace of contemporary American family life is eroding family closeness and depriving our children of their childhood, and because we know something about how to take back family time and make good use of it. Today's families, we believe, are sorely lacking time for spontaneous fun and enjoyment, for talking over the day's events and experiences, for unhurried meals, for quiet bedtime talks, for working together on projects, for teaching and learning life skills such as cooking and gardening, for visiting extended family and friends, for attending religious services together, for participating together in community projects, and for exploring the beauty of nature. Not enough time, that is, to be a family with a rich internal and external life.

There are many contributors to the "time famine" experienced by many families, including parents' work commitments, employers' expectations for increased work hours, and larger economic forces. Some of these forces can be controlled by individual families and others cannot. Our focus in this book is on something that parents can control: the problem of overscheduling children in a competitive culture. You might not have much say when your employer insists that you work extra hours, to the detriment of your family time. But you do have a say as to whether your child takes up a second musical instrument or joins a traveling sports team. You might not have control over whether you can be home for dinner reliably at six o'clock, but your family can decide to snack early and then eat later in the evening when you can all be together. When you are scheduling your summer, you might not be able to claim the exact weeks for vacation that you would prefer, but you can hold sacred the vacation time you do have—and not surrender it to the vagaries of children's baseball schedules or enrichment French lessons.

There is strong talk in this book about what we have lost in our families and about how our children are becoming harried preadults. You may feel regret or guilt at times as you read along. You may have surrendered your family dinners to overscheduling and television watching. You may not have created bedtime rituals for your children because you don't need the hassle of getting them to bed. A certain amount of regret and guilt comes with the territory of being a caring parent, because we all make mistakes. But two ideas in this book can help to offset the guilt and turn it into constructive action. First, the problems we are talking about are rooted in the broader culture we have created together; they are not primarily the fault of individual parents. Second, the solutions, both personal and communal, are within our grasp if we reach for them. We are not talking about solving an intractable social problem such as world poverty or ethnic hatred. We can do something right now, in our own lives and with our neighbors, about the problem of overscheduled kids and underconnected families. We can take back our kids and renew our family time.

You will find our own family stories in the pages of this book. We bring different life paths and common values to the writing. Bill is a professor, a marriage and family therapist, and a community activist. He has been married to his wife, Leah, since 1971 and has two grown children, Eric (born in 1973) and Elizabeth (born in 1975). He is aware of having raised them in the simpler era of the 1970s and 1980s, before the invasion of hyperscheduling of kids' outside activities. Barbara's learning has come primarily from work in the "trenches" as a mother, elementary teacher, high-school service learning director, community organizer, and volunteer. Barbara and Sam have been married since 1970 and have shared the parenting of Angela (born in 1973), twins Adam and Laura (1977), and Joshua (1983). Barbara is learning wonderful new skills as a mother-in-law from Matthew and Britt.

Beyond our own experiences, this book comes out of a

grass-roots parents initiative we have been part of since 1999— Putting Family First, based in Wayzata, Minnesota. Putting Family First is a group of citizens building a community where family life is an honored and celebrated priority—and not an afterthought when there is free space on the activity schedule. The public visibility of the Putting Family First initiative and its message, beginning with a *New York Times* article in June 2000, led to the idea of a book project. We want to acknowledge our fellow members of Putting Family First as coinspirers of what is in these pages, and in particular we want to thank the following members who read and commented on an earlier draft: Carol Bergenstal, Gina Coburn, John Holst, Sue Kakuk, Bugs Peterschmidt, Amanda Richards, and Carol Vannelli. A number of their own stories appear in this book, along with stories from dozens of other parents.

❦

Along with our fellow citizens, we will be processing for many years the meaning of the events of September 11, 2001. But our first conclusion is this: everything has changed and nothing has changed. We have awakened as from a slumber to the sobering new world of the twenty-first century, where the risks and the rules are different. But we have also realized anew something we have known all along, something we lost sight of in our high-speed, consumerist culture: close families, immersed in vibrant democratic communities, have always been the source of our strength as a people.

Putting Family First

It's Time for Action:
Overscheduled Kids,
Underconnected Families

At 3:00 P.M., school is out in Pompton Plains, New Jersey, and the Scofield family has begun its round of after-school activities. Fourteen-year-old Annie is in band practice. Across town, her eleven-year-old brother, Tim, is doing his homework in the car, while waiting with Mom until six-year-old sister, Teresa, is finished with school. Then it's a quick drive home for a snack, and more homework for Tim.

At 4:00 P.M., Annie is in cheerleading practice, while Teresa is in gymnastics. At 4:45, Mom, Annie, and Tim have a fast dinner. Fifteen minutes later, Dad returns from work and grabs dinner from what is left over. Then he's off with Annie to a voice lesson. Timmy leaves for baseball practice. Then Teresa arrives home from gymnastics and has dinner on her own, with Mom having coffee at the table. Then she starts her homework.

At 6:00, Teresa has a piano lesson. At 6:25, Annie returns and goes straight to her piano lesson. At 6:45, Tim has religion class. At 7:45, Annie is doing her homework. Teresa is ready for bed. Dad warmly but efficiently says good night and tucks her in. At

8:30, Tim is now home, and the kids' eight combined activities are over for the day.

Although not every day is this busy, the Scofields are a typical American family trying to make the most out of childhood. When asked about her rationale for this family lifestyle, the mother explains, "The kids have a schedule, and we like to keep them active and busy." Why so many activities? "We want our kids to be happy," she states confidently. "We want them to be well-rounded. They seem well-adjusted. And we think we're doing a pretty good job." When questioned about whether the kids' schedules are too crowded, she responds perhaps a bit defensively, "They like these things. It's not like we're forcing them to go."

Frantic families like this one are all around us. Well-intentioned parents are acting like recreation directors on a turbo-charged family cruise ship. Children are involved in soccer, hockey, piano, Boy Scouts and Girl Scouts, baseball, football, karate, gymnastics, dance, violin, band, craft clubs, foreign language classes, academic enrichment courses, and religious youth activities. Family life today revolves around children's activities rather than these activities revolving around the family's schedule. It wasn't this way before. The cart and the horse have switched positions in the last two decades, with hardly anyone noticing until recently. Families now have schedules previously seen only in presidential campaigns.

Many parents mourn the older priorities about family time but feel helpless to get off today's merry-go-round. We hear parents complain about running all the time, having dinner in the car between practices, and missing out on summer vacations because of sports tournaments and specialized camps. Although children get used to whatever family life they are raised in, we are beginning to hear them ask to slow down. Six-year-olds get their first daily planners, and then ask for time to just play. A nine-year-old boy, in his top-ten list of birthday presents, placed "more time at home" as number three. Twelve-year-olds sheepishly ask their parents if it's okay not to try out for the traveling soccer team. Grandparents wonder why they cannot get on their grandchildren's crowded dance cards. One grandfather shared with sadness that the only way he gets to see his grandson is from the stands at hockey games.

When various outside activities compete with one another—as they generally do—things really get crazy for today's families. Reflecting our competitive culture, many of us want excellence for our children in every area. And each activity leader—coach, music teacher, schoolteacher, youth religious director—feels that his or her own activity requires a good deal of time and commitment. So kids are torn between hockey practice and confirmation classes, between homework and violin practice, between cheerleading and the fall musical. In the face of these competing demands, family activities like dinners, weekend outings, vacations, and visits to relatives are the first priorities to go. We end up with overscheduled and underconnected families. Though overwhelmed, we still don't think we are doing enough for our children.

What is going on here? First, some facts. According to a national survey conducted by the University of Michigan's Survey Research Center, since the late 1970s people in the United States have experienced a remarkable change in children's schedules and family activities. Children have lost twelve hours per week in free time, including a 25 percent drop in playing and a 50 percent drop in unstructured outdoor activities. During the same period, time in structured sports has doubled, and passive, spectator leisure (watching others play and perform, but not including television) increased from thirty minutes per week to over three hours. In other words, children make up their own play activities a lot less often, engage in supervised sports a lot more often, and spend a whole lot more time watching passively from the sidelines.

It isn't just that children are busier; families spend less time together. According to the same survey, household conversations between parents and children—time for just talking—have dropped nearly off the radar screen, and there has been a 28 percent decline in the number of families taking vacations. Other national surveys have found a one-third decrease in the number of families who say they have family dinners regularly.

This change in American family life is deep and broad, cutting a wide swath across income groups and ethnic groups in the population. (The very poor do not have the resources to be overscheduled but they face similar challenges in finding time to connect as a family.) And it has come upon us with amazing speed. But is this change unwelcome? Is it a problem, or just an inevitable part of modern life? We believe it's a serious problem. If you listen to parents, as we do, you know that many feel burdened by crammed schedules and feel a severe loss of family connections. If you listen to teachers, as we do, you know that they see a generation of students weary from schedules that even many adults couldn't handle. A woman from a community near Albany, New York, a teacher of second graders for thirty years, used strong language: "This is an abused generation," she said at a public meeting. She went on to explain that, after thirty years of teaching the same age group, she has never seen children so tired and burdened from being up too early in the morning, going to bed too late at night, and being crunched in between by extremely competitive activities. And hers is a privileged, upper-middle-class community.

The National Association of Elementary School Principals is now weighing in on the problem of overscheduled children. It has issued a recommendation of one activity at a time for young children, with that activity meeting only once or twice a week. If you want your child to experience more than one activity, the association recommends different activities season by season, rather than more than one activity in a single season. These recommendations seem wildly far off from the current schedules of many children and families.

The effects of overbusy family life on child development are just beginning to be studied by academic researchers. But studies have shown the importance of regular family dinners, one of the chief casualties of hyperscheduling. A large national study of American teenagers found a strong link between regular family meals and a wide range of positive outcomes: academic success, psychological adjustment, and lower rates of alcohol use, drug use, early sexual behavior, and suicidal risk. On the flip side, not having regular family meals was associated with higher risks in all of those areas.

This study defined a family meal as one in which the teenager ate with at least one parent. Given the documented decline in family dinners, it is not surprising that a national poll of teenagers, funded by the White House in spring 2000, found that over one-fifth of American teens rated "not having enough time with parents" as their top concern, a percentage that tied for first (along with education) on their list of worries.

We also know that children who eat dinner regularly with their families do better nutritionally. One study found that these children have more healthful dietary patterns in a number of areas: more fruits and vegetables, less saturated fat, fewer fried foods and sodas, and more foods rich in vitamins and other micronutrients. Like the other study cited above, these findings held across family income levels.

Something is out of whack in American family life, but it's not because parents are enrolling their children in bad activities. We know from common sense and a lot of research that extracurricular involvement is good for kids. Sports, music, other fine arts, and religious involvement—all of these contribute to a rich life for a child. The issue is one of balance. And balance requires setting priorities. In our view, there is a serious imbalance and a confused set of priorities in the raising of this generation of children.

How Did We Get Here?

It is easier to document the problem of overscheduled kids and underconnected families than it is to explain how it came upon us. There are many explanations, many factors contributing to the problem, and not one decisive cause. We have asked hundreds of parents at community events for their explanations for the social change we have described. Here is what they say, followed by our own synthesis of the reasons why we are facing a problem of over-scheduled kids and underconnected families.

• *More opportunities for children, especially for girls.* There are more activities to choose from today than twenty years ago. One mother in Northfield, Minnesota, said that she counted fourteen community activities for three-year-olds. Another mother stressed that she wants her daughters to take advantage of sports opportunities that were not available to her when she was growing up.

• *More intense sports activities.* Sports used to be seasonal; now many are year-round. Traveling teams were unheard-of twenty-five years ago, outside of varsity sports. As one veteran coach told us, we have lost the distinction between competitive sports and recreational sports. And this has spilled over to activities such as dance programs and gymnastics, which travel to compete. Practices for all kinds of activities now occur three or more times per week, with weekend competitions. And this happens for children as young as seven!

- *Competition for sports facilities and performance halls.* This means invasion of family time. Take hockey, for example. Limited ice facilities combined with high demand means that some kids practice at 6 A.M. or 10 P.M. The burden on soccer fields means that many teams play on Sunday morning. Music and academic programs require numerous practices and rehearsals as well. And dinner gives way to swimming, music, basketball, and all the rest.

- *More working parents.* Parents need to fill children's time after school with structured activities. Of course, this does not explain the overscheduling of evening and weekend hours. Nor does it explain why families with a stay-at-home parent are often as frantic as families with two working parents or a single parent working outside the home.

- *Parental guilt.* Parents who themselves feel too busy with work or other activities do not want to deprive their children of any worthwhile opportunity. One mother with a full-time professional job told us that she was determined that her children would not miss out on any opportunities because of her career. She then admitted that the family rarely has dinner together and has a crazed schedule.

- *Overreaction to the message that kids do better if they are busy and involved in the community.* The word has gotten out to parents that structured outside activities get children involved with other adults and expand their horizons beyond staying home and watching television. What those messages do not emphasize is when to say "enough." And missing entirely is the message that even good outside activities come with a cost to family life.

- *Sense of danger in the neighborhood.* Many parents remember being allowed to play freely in the neighborhood as children, but keep their own children at home or in structured activities because of unsafe neighborhoods. These fears are no doubt well-founded in some neighborhoods, but often extend to areas where violent crime is rare or nonexistent.

• *Fear that one's child will miss out or be left behind.* This fuels early, intense involvement in activities, with parents worrying that delaying the start of a sport or musical instrument may doom their child to not being able to play competitively at all in the future.

• *Increased emphasis on what very young children are capable of.* The preschool years now receive far more emphasis in child development, and parents feel a cultural expectation to get their preschoolers involved in enriching activities. One mother of a four-year-old said that she is getting the message from friends and relatives that her daughter (whom the friends and relatives see as athletic) is already behind in gymnastics because she did not start at age three.

• *Pressure on contemporary children to "succeed."* From having to know the alphabet and colors before going to school, to worrying about a college résumé in sixth grade, to having to compete at high levels in athletics, this is a generation of children and parents who are preoccupied with visible signs of success.

• *The expectations of elite colleges for "well-rounded" applicants.* During the 1980s and 1990s, these colleges began to emphasize the breadth of students' nonacademic record. High-school students responded by an explosion of activities designed to beef up their résumés. One sport was not enough, or one musical instrument, or just one leadership position in the school. Community service became a must, with yearbook editorship on the side. Interestingly, in the fall of 2000, Harvard's admissions office published a report saying, in effect, Enough! We've created a monster. The report described arriving students who are decidedly not well-rounded and who are already burned out when they enter college.

• *Parental peer pressure.* All of the forces we've mentioned tend to influence parents most strongly through their peers, that is, from parents of children of similar ages. Parents watch other parents and listen to what other parents say. Look at how holiday letters glowingly describe the plethora of activities the children are involved in. How many say that the family is in more balance this year, spending more time together? And look at the parental pressure on the sidelines at sports events. One father recounts how another father quietly bragged that his son made the traveling soccer team and was also planning to go out for baseball. Then came the question, "Is your son going to be on the traveling team?" Fortunately, the first father could answer yes, but had to answer no to the follow-up question about the boy going out for baseball. The other father smiled and asked, "Is he not good at baseball?" Later, when the son decided to quit traveling soccer in favor of a less intense league, his parents worried that he lacked the competitive edge to be successful in life.

All of these factors, and more, contribute to the problem. But what's the big picture? We believe that the adult world of hyper-competition and marketplace values has invaded the family. Parents of course love their children and try to do what is best for them. But we are raising our children in a culture that defines a good parent as an opportunity provider in a competitive world. Parenting becomes like product development, with insecure parents never knowing when they've done enough and when their children are falling behind. Keeping our children busy at least means they are in the game.

A parent told us recently that in her upper-middle-class community, people no longer brag about the size of their house or the model of their car—they brag about how busy their family is. When one parent, in mock complaint, says, "We're so busy right now," another parent tops it with a more extreme story. And in a market-oriented, money-driven culture, we can point more readily to things we pay for—equipment, registration fees, traveling expenses, coaches' salaries—than for low-key family activities like hanging out together on a Sunday afternoon or playing a board game on a Friday night. It's the same with children's playtime: we don't easily assign ourselves "parent points" for providing our children with time to daydream and make up games to play with the neighbor kids. Parenting has become a competitive sport, with the trophies going to the busiest.

Managing Your Schedule to Put Family Life First

Now that we have set up the problem and explained why we think it has overtaken us as a society, the rest of the book will focus on what you can do in your own family and your own community to find balance in your life. Here is what you can expect out of this book.

We will begin by inviting you to ask yourself what you value about family life, then look carefully, maybe even painfully, at how you are using your time. Based on examples from families in our community, we will show you how to assess your current family lifestyle. When you have said yes too often to new activities and opportunities, saying no can be an unfamiliar challenge. We will encourage you to make the changes that you want to make. We offer no prescriptions for your family, just lots of encouragement and plenty of strategies, based on actual families' experiences, for turning your family ship in the direction you want to be heading.

The first big priority we will focus on is family meals, which can be the first beachhead for reclaiming family life. Then we will move on to bedtime rituals, time to hang out, family outings and vacations, and how to manage television and the Internet in order to preserve family time. Then we will discuss making family life a priority in different family forms that have unique challenges: two-parent families, single-parent families, and stepfamilies, with an additional chapter on preserving time for a marriage while raising children. All along the way, we will tell you the stories we have gathered from families about how they have found balance in a frantic world.

The problems we are addressing are community and cultural problems as well as individual family problems. The solutions therefore must be both personal and communal. In the last part of the book, we will talk about how to take charge and make changes in your own family. And we will talk about community solutions such as the Putting Family First movement, a democratic, parent-led initiative to change how parents and communities prioritize family life.

The Tide Is Turning Back to the Family

While the Scofield family of Pompton Plains, New Jersey, may be typical today, we believe that the next cultural wave is calling us all back to making putting family first in our lives. Here is a day in the life of the Peterschmidt family, from Plymouth, Minnesota, who have been active with us in creating the Putting Family First initiative.

The Peterschmidts used to be as busy as the Scofields, the family whose day we chronicled at the beginning of this chapter. But recently the Peterschmidts have cut back on after-school activities. At 3:00, twelve-year-old Max is finished with school and has one scheduled activity, a violin lesson. Nine-year-old Betsy goes to a friend's house to play for the rest of the afternoon. By 5:15, both children are home and have playtime together before dinner. At 6 P.M., Dad arrives home; he had left for work early in the morning to make sure he was home for dinner. Mom also works, but is able to be home when the children get home from school.

At 6:15, the family dines together, always by candlelight. Then it's homework, individual activities, some television decided upon in advance, and a bedtime talk.

The father explained, "We want them to be active in things, but it's being too active where we saw a problem occurring." Mom added, "Everyone doesn't have a big to-do list everyday anymore. We have more flexibility." She went on. "I think it's hard being a kid. It's exhausting work to play and learn. I don't think anybody can be effective in any type of skill if you're tired. And now that they're rested, it's just made a world of difference. It's been the easiest school year so far, because we're not tired. We've not taken everything out; we've prioritized."

That's what this book is about: priorities, setting them and living by them in a hyperbusy, competitive culture that is pulling our families apart faster than love and goodwill alone can hold them together.

2

It's About Time:
Putting First Things First

Wherever we go in the country, we hear the same refrain from parents: my family's schedule is out of control, but I don't know what I can do about it. Competent adults who can take charge of other important areas of their life—finding the right job, the right school for their children, the right stores to shop in—feel helpless when they think about getting off the treadmill they have created for themselves and their children.

Take the Friedrickson family. Marilee, the mother, knows that her family is out of balance. We won't bore you with the specifics— it's the standard fare of multiple sports, musical instruments, dance, and religion classes, on top of busy adult schedules. The tipping point for Marilee came this fall when her eight-year-old daughter, Jessica, enrolled in two sports at the same time. Why did Marilee and her husband allow it? Because Jessica really wanted to try soccer in addition to gymnastics, and they wanted to reward her initiative. When kids want to push themselves, today's parents are afraid to stifle this initiative, despite the costs.

So now Jessica is too busy and the family is on the merry-go-round. Why not just eliminate one of the activities? Marilee says that she is afraid to do this—afraid that Jessica will fall behind her peers, that she will fail to develop herself in an important area. Marilee asked, "What if my daughter's gifts are in an activity that we deny her? Maybe the next thing she wants to do is the one where she will excel. What if Michael Jordan's parents had not let him play basketball?"

Marilee knew that she sounded a bit foolish when she compared her daughter to Michael Jordan. But she was honestly expressing feelings and fears that many other parents keep to themselves. She was driven not so much by ambition for her daughter to be a future superstar, but by anxiety about not doing enough for her child. The irony is that this mother was not anxious enough about the real risk facing Jessica: that she would miss out on a balanced childhood and a rich and deep family life.

We have never talked to a parent who did not believe that solid family bonds are the most important factor in a child's life. National polls taken over many decades report the same belief: American adults say they place the highest value on family life— over money, health, religion, and everything else. Even studies of elderly people who started out as gifted children show that these individuals rate success in family life as more important than any other accomplishment. We also know from a large body of academic research that close family connections, with lots of warmth combined with effective limits, are the cornerstone of successful child development. Nothing that erodes the time vitally necessary to sustain these bonds can be good for children or families. In raising children, family life is first—period.

Marilee and her husband believe all of this. As we said, almost no one disagrees. The problem is not what we believe about family life; it's how we set priorities, how we make choices in a world that pulls us in so many directions. And no choice is more crucial for family life today than how we spend our time.

We Are How We Spend Our Time

A teacher recently told us about an amazing encounter with a nine-year-old boy in her class. The teacher was telling the boy that he had to clean up after himself at his library table. He snapped at her, "I don't have time for this!" We suspect that this kind of response is new in the annals of childhood. Another teacher told of a six-year-old girl who started to cry one day while waiting for her mother to pick her up after school. Years ago, we would have assumed there was a problem at home; maybe her parents were breaking up or she was being abused. In truth, she was dreading spending the next five hours in a car racing after a frantic series of activities. She just wanted to go home.

Advertisers know a trend when they see one. On one television commercial we see a father deciding to visit his young son's room. Upon opening the door, he is confronted by a stern, gray-haired woman sitting at an office desk just inside the door. "May I help you?" she inquires curtly. "Is Bobby here?" the befuddled father asks. "And *you* are . . . ?" she replies. "I'm his father!" he retorts. "Do you have an appointment?" she demands.

Another ad shows a hectic mom on her cell phone pacing the floor as she schedules numerous meetings. With eyes pleading, her young daughter approaches the mom and asks, "Mommy, when can *we* have a meeting?"

As the last vignettes indicate, one reason why so many families experience time famine is that parents are working more hours outside the home. We live in an era of dual-working families and employed single-parent families. A consequence is less time for children, especially in the late-afternoon time period, and more busyness on evenings and weekends when employed parents must do their errands and chores. Studies show that since 1960 children have lost ten to twelve hours per week of time with their parents. Of course, there have been many benefits for families from mothers entering the workforce, and many parents make good use of less time. We are not proposing that the clock be turned back to the 1950s family. But more parental work hours mean that families have to be better at setting priorities than families in the past. If we overschedule our children on top of our own work and personal schedules, we've got a big mess.

Sometimes parents make the valid point that they do spend a lot of time with their children, driving them to and from activities. What's more, being on the sidelines at games is a way to connect with your child. Weekend trips for traveling teams, doing Suzuki lessons together, teaching religious education to your child's class—these are all ways to connect. In fact, some parents argue that they spend more time with their children doing these kinds of activities than their own parents spent with them as children.

A group of mothers in a central Pennsylvania community have an unspoken norm that they will not carpool their daughters to soccer games, even when the games are ninety minutes away, because it is important to spend that time one-on-one with their daughters. A new mother in the community discovered this norm when she came to the meeting place before her daughter's first game and asked about taking turns driving the girls to away games. She was met with stern stares and statements that each parent drives her own child to all games.

Many of these contemporary parents would concede that they don't have many family dinners, family outings, bedtime talks, unstructured family time, and visits to relatives. But they feel they are better cheerleaders and supporters for their own children than their parents were for them, and may spend more of a different kind of time with their own children.

When we talk to these parents, we are quick to affirm their commitment to their children's well-being. And we agree that chauffeuring time and cheerleading time can be valuable. Some important, spontaneous conversations occur in the car as nowhere else. It's great to be there for our children's successes and failures in their activities. But we think that these parents are emphasizing one kind of time over other kinds of time that are perhaps more important.

We like to think of three different ways of being with children. See if this breakdown makes sense to you in your own life.

Family Time: "Being Around"

The first way to spend time with children is "being around." Being around is when you are near your children, accessible to them, but not necessarily communicating directly with them. You may be cooking, cleaning, reading the newspaper, watching television, driving them in the car, or watching them practice gymnastics or violin. This is the basic building block of family life; nothing substitutes for enough time just being around one another. Babies and young children need oodles of it; a baby will crawl from room to room to find its parent. Older children and teenagers need somewhat less, but still depend on our presence and accessibility. A large national study of teenagers showed that teens want to connect with their parents at four time periods each day: when they get up in the morning, when they get home from school, at dinner, and when they go to bed. Being teens, they may not always want to talk to them, but they want them to be available if *they* decide to talk.

Except for time spent in jobs, contemporary parents may have as much being-around time as previous generations. It's not that parents are indulging in personal hobbies instead of being with their children. But we spend that time in more hurried activities than in the past. (Ask yourself how often you tell your children to hurry up.) We drive them through rush-hour traffic to their piano lesson, with the car radio giving traffic reports. Less often do we sit on the front porch, or throw a ball back and forth in the yard, or play a leisurely game of Monopoly. Being around, and unhurried, is the first key to having enough family time. Later we will devote a chapter to hanging out as a family.

Family Time: Logistics Talk

As we said, being around does not necessarily involve conversation. When we do talk with our children, the biggest category of communication is what we call "logistics talk" or "getting-things-done talk." Think about the bulk of what you say to your children every day. Doesn't most of it take the form of giving them information and directives, asking them matter-of-fact questions, and saying yes or no to their requests? Here is how a regular day's conversation goes on our end as parents:

• "Time to get up for school. . . . Get dressed now. . . . Your breakfast is ready. . . . The bus will be coming soon. . . . Don't forget your schoolbag."

• "No, you cannot wear that lightweight outfit in this cold weather. . . . I don't have time to make French toast today. . . . Don't forget your permission slip for the field trip; is it in your bag? Hurry up, the bus is coming!"

• "After you get home, here's a snack you can eat before you go to your piano lesson. . . . Apologize to Mrs. Garfield for not practicing this week. . . . I'll pick you up there for soccer. . . . Hurry up and get in the car."

• "What do you want for supper? No, we don't have frozen burritos. . . . It will have to be hamburgers. . . . Please remember to chew with your mouth closed. . . . Stop making fun of your sister. . . . No, we don't have ice cream. . . . Time for homework; do you need any help? When is your science project due? Have you asked your father for help with it? Get moving, it's time for bed."

• "No, you cannot wear that top with those jeans because your belly button shows and it's twenty degrees outside!"

• "Time to turn off the TV and get ready for bed. . . . I mean it—get ready for bed. You're going to be tired in the morning if you don't get to sleep. . . . All right, I'll read you a quick story."

Logistics conversations are what makes a family function in its everyday routines. They can be done pleasantly or unpleasantly, but they must be done nonetheless. They make the family business run. It's the same way with marriage: everyday scheduling and where's-the-gas-bill conversations dominate marital exchanges. As necessary as logistics talk is, though, it alone does not bring much depth of feeling to family life. It's not why we had kids.

Family Time: Connecting Talk

What gets squeezed by hurried schedules and logistics are opportunities for what we call "connecting talk." It's what happens when we are focused on our child and the conversation, and not on something else. When Bill's children were young, his favorite connecting times were bedtime rituals, when he and his kids would talk, sing, read, play hide-under-the-covers, and cuddle. As they got older and could carry their weight in family conversation, dinnertime became another important opportunity for family connection. He and his wife tried to avoid logistics talk at dinner, and instead talked about what happened during everyone's day.

Connecting time is personal time. It's about you and your child, about what is on your or your child's mind. It's about what your child is feeling or has experienced. It's about stories of the day, about thoughts, values, insights, fears, and hopes. A simple but powerful type of connecting conversation occurs over a snack after school as a parent looks through a seven-year-old's schoolbag and they talk about the child's artwork or the exciting field trip coming up the next day. There is no logistical purpose to the conversation, although certain news gets shared. No directives are given. It's a time for reconnection after the school day.

Connecting talk happens most reliably when you build in special time for it every day in your family's schedule, times like getting up in the morning, after school, during dinner, at bedtime, or on a weekend outing. It requires relief from time pressures, at least for a little while, so that people can settle into being together. But connecting talk can also happen spontaneously during being-around time. Barbara remembers her daughter storming through the front door after school one day. She was not in a mood to talk, but noted that her mother was around. After stomping off to her room, she returned in three minutes, ready to pour out her heart about her best friend, who had just abandoned her for the new girl in the class. Because Barbara was around, "on call" if you will, and ready to connect, her daughter took the opportunity for an important conversation.

Bill remembers how as a teenager his son, Eric, would, from time to time, walk into his home office in the evening and say, "How's my dad?" Bill would turn his chair away from the computer, put his feet up on a table, and reply, "Fine. How's my son?" This was Eric's signal that he wanted to talk. With teenagers in particular, you have to have enough time to hang around for these spontaneous connecting conversations to occur.

The gulf between our values about family life and our everyday experience is most apparent in our lack of connecting conversations. Many of us are spending every available nonworking, nonsleeping moment doing things for and with our children. But too much of this time is hurried being-around time and fast-paced logistics talk. What most of us need, in order to better align our priorities with our core values, is more unhurried time with our children and more personal connection. Meeting this need requires taking a hard look at how we are spending our time now.

Looking Hard at Your Priorities

The old Beatles song, "All You Need Is Love," could not be more wrong when it comes to parenting. Love for our children is the starting point, but the rest depends a lot on how we set priorities for our time with them. We encourage you to ask yourself whether you have enough being-around time with your children (especially unhurried time) and whether you have enough connecting time with them. Logistics time tends to take care of itself. Take the following quiz to determine if your family is overscheduled.

In thinking about how much time is enough, keep in mind that this will differ for different families. A good place to start is to ask yourself about your core values about family life. How close do you hope your family will be? What do you think about the balance between family time and individual time, between family solidarity and individual opportunity? How much do you see your family as a launching pad versus a nest? How important are family meals to you, aside from the need for adequate nutrition for your children? How important are other rituals such as visits to grandparents, vacations, bedtime talks, and weekend outings? In other words, ask yourself what kind of family life you aspire to. If you are in a two-parent family, ask your spouse the same questions to see how much you are in accord.

Are You a Frantic Family?

Answering these questions can help you decide if your family is overscheduled.

1. We struggle to find time for unhurried family meals.
   True   False
2. I think we spend too much time getting to and from our children's activities.
   True   False
3. Homework can be difficult to squeeze into the children's schedules.
   True   False
4. My kids don't have enough time to hang out and entertain themselves.
   True   False
5. I wish we spent more time home as a family.
   True   False
6. It is hard to visit with relatives and family friends because we are so busy.
   True   False
7. We don't go on family trips and outings as much as we would like.
   True   False
8. Even on weekends it can be hard to get the whole family together because of everyone's schedules.
   True   False

Scoring: Give yourself 1 point for each true answer. Add up your points. If your total is 6–8, you are probably a seriously frantic family. If your total is 3–5, you are probably a somewhat frantic family. If 0–2, congratulations and please teach the rest of us how you do it!

Then ask yourself what you believe your children need in terms of unhurried being-around time and connection time. Depending on their ages and personalities, some children need more or less from you. You might want to ask them what they like most about time with their family. Walk them through a typical day or week and ask how they feel about, say, having you around after school, or having family dinners, or bedtime talks. You might be surprised about what they say. However, as the leader of the family, you cannot simply rely on your children's preferences. Sometimes they get used to a hurried, unconnected pace of family life and might not understand what they are missing when, for example, they never have experienced slowed-down Sunday dinners or regular family meals. Teens might not voluntarily sign up for more connecting time. Children should not be treated like customers who always know what they need in family life.

Next comes the hardest part. Ask yourself if your family's current schedule allows you enough time for what is most important. If there is a gap, what are its sources? If you are too hurried with your children, what in your schedule creates the rush? If you are lacking enough connecting time, what is getting in the way? Is it sheer lack of hours or are you not using your time well? For example, is too much at-home time spent watching television in separate rooms? Is your work schedule a problem, or your spouse's? Is it your children's outside schedules or homework responsibilities?

Until recently, professionals too have overlooked the problem of overscheduled kids and underconnected families. Like individual families, many professionals have focused so much on the importance of outside activities to bolster children's self-esteem and sense of mastery that they have missed what is obvious: family life is first. A long list of activities becomes the marker of a young person who will achieve and stay out of trouble. Let's be clear: community involvement is essential for children and youth, but not as a substitute for family time.

FIGURE 2.1

Time Priorities Pyramid

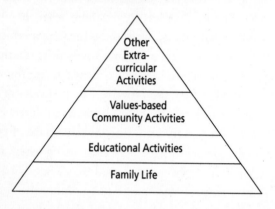

We see time priorities for children and families as a pyramid (like the food pyramid for nutritional guidelines). In our view, family time is at the base of the pyramid. Above this foundation comes time spent in learning or educational activities. The next most important time priority would be religious or value-based activities, and then other extracurricular activities such as sports. There is time in most children's lives for activities at all levels, but with clear priorities. (See our view of this pyramid of time priorities in Figure 2.1.) You might order some of the time priorities differently than we do, and the amount of family time will change as children get older. But in any priority system, we believe that meaningful family time (especially connecting time) is still the base of child development.

We suspect you would not have picked up this book if you felt that your schedule permits all the unhurried being-around time and connection time that your family needs. Chances are your family has caught the "busy virus" of contemporary life and that you would like to do something about it. If you sense there is a gap between your family values and your everyday experience of family life, you are part of a very large group. That means that there are plenty of us around to figure out how to bridge the distance between what we value and how we are living.

But it is not enough just to reclaim family time for being together and connecting. Many of us have to learn, or relearn, how to use this time. That's where we turn next, beginning with family meals.

3

This Kitchen Is Not a Pit Stop: Reclaiming Family Meals

Dinnertime was the centerpiece of the Graham family's life. High-energy conversations, good-natured teasing, everyone pitching in, time to linger before cleanup—and the food wasn't bad either! They had their moments of irritation during dinner, but mostly you could tell that this family really liked being together and sharing a meal. Then the Grahams lost their family dinners without anyone even noticing.

Let's back up a bit before describing the decline and fall of the Graham family dinners. The family consisted of two employed parents and their three children, Jon (eleven), Nathan (nine), and Lisa (seven). Dad worked the early shift as a nurse and was home when the children got home from school. He was the main cook in the family. Mom, who was a teacher, did the grocery shopping and menu planning. The three children took turns setting the table and helping with cleanup, and on Sunday mornings Nathan often made pancakes for the family. A high-energy clan, their dinners were a source of pride, a feeling that guests easily picked up on.

And then came competitive swimming. The kids must have received their mother's athletic genes, because they were all terrific athletes for their age. After several years of low-key swim teams, their parents moved them up to a more intense level that required three practices per week, a meet every weekend, and regular travel out of town. And of course their teams practiced on different days and at different times! The family's late-afternoon and early-evening schedule became a whirl of car rides, drop-offs, and pickups. Except for Tuesday evening, when everyone was home, dinner became a pit stop. Dad left food in the refrigerator for the kids to pick up and chow down. Sometimes one parent and two children would eat together, but for the most part both parents were not together at dinner, and only on Tuesday (and Sunday) was there the possibility of the whole family being together. Then Tuesday dinners were lost to a special band practice for Lisa, who was the most musical member of the family. Her parents did not want Lisa to miss out on an opportunity available only to a small number of children in the community.

Sunday dinners remained, but even there, something had been lost. High energy had ratcheted up a notch toward chaos as the children moved to and away from the table, complained more about the food, elicited more reprimands from the parents, and asked to leave the table as soon as they finished their food. The spirit was not the same.

Being a good friend of the family, Bill decided to ask everyone separately if they had noticed the change and how they felt about it. A year into this new schedule, the two older children said that they had not noticed the decline in the number of family dinners. When Bill pointed out that they used to have dinners as a family nearly all the time, and wondered if they missed them, Jon reflected a bit and said, "Yeah, I kind of like being together as a family." But then he added, "But I like just eating what I want to." Nathan was less positive, claiming, "It's boring eating as a family; I'd rather play one of my video games while I eat." Lisa didn't have much to say during Bill's brief conversation with the children.

The mother, for her part, missed family dinners very much and worried about the family being on a fast treadmill. The father focused on how much the children were deriving from swimming and how dedicated they were to it. He also stressed the quality time the parents had individually with the children in the car. And he mentioned that swimming was only six months of the year, a point that the mother countered by noting that soccer filled the rest of the year.

The Graham family is unusual only because the decline of their dinner ritual was so steep and fast. They are like many families nowadays, though, in having their dinner rituals erode without much notice or regret from most family members, although there is often one member, the mother in this case, who feels the loss. If your family is like the Grahams', we offer ideas for reclaiming your family meals and making them connecting rituals. If not, we want to help you hold on to your meal rituals and enhance them.

What's the Big Deal About Family Meals?

Our bodies are designed by nature to get hungry at least three times a day. And we are social creatures who generally prefer to eat with others. (Think about how we apologize for eating food in front of someone who is not eating, and how we almost always invite that person to share our food.) All cultural practices and major religions in the world have meal rituals at their core.

Before we talk more about meal rituals, it's time for us to say what we mean by a family ritual. Basically, a ritual is a coordinated activity that the family does over and over and has emotional meaning to family members. To qualify as a ritual, the activity must be repeated over time—from daily events like bedtime talks to an annual event like a vacation. The activity must be organized enough that people know when it is happening and how to act during it (think of birthday parties).

The difference between a routine and a ritual is that a ritual has the extra element of emotional significance. A routine would be how bathroom visits are organized every morning in a large family—repeated, coordinated, but not especially significant! A ritual would be a nightly bath a parent gives a young child, when they play together and enjoy each other. Rituals can involve the whole family, subgroups in the family (like one parent and one child), the extended family, or the family and its larger community.

Family meals are the central daily ritual opportunity in family life. At their best, they are an oasis in a hectic day, a time to reconnect, relax, discuss, debate, support one another, and laugh together. Family dinners in particular are apt to be the only time during the day when the whole family has the chance to be together, face-to-face, doing the same activity and sharing in conversation. The rest of the time, we are mostly involved in solo or one-to-one activities. Family dinner rituals involve all three uses of family time that we discussed earlier:

- *Being around,* as we prepare meals, set up, eat our food, and clean up
- *Logistics talk,* as we use the meal to catch up on what is happening on everyone's schedule
- *Connecting talk,* as we use the meal (at the best of times, anyway) to tell stories, share opinions and feelings, and generally get caught up on one another's lives.

Meal rituals are where the family culture is created and nurtured. It doesn't have to be dinner; we know families who have breakfast together and others who make a big deal of Sunday brunch. And a family who simply cannot have meals together might be able to create an equally valuable alternative ritual of family connection. But it's a challenge to create a viable substitute for the simple act of eating dinner together most days.

Earlier in the book we described research supporting the importance of family dinners. Children and adolescents do better in almost all areas of life when their families have regular dinners. Nutritionists have found that meals prepared at home mean better nourishment, lower-fat diets, and less harried consumption. Opinion polls reveal that the public believes in family dinners. But if almost everyone now agrees about the value of family dinners (and other meals), why do good families give them up and find it so hard to reclaim them?

Family Dinners:
A Much-Loved But Endangered Species

The Graham family holds some of the clues to why family dinners are so difficult to pull off nowadays. Most families have dual-earner couples or single parents; in either case, one parent does not have a lot of time for meal planning and preparation. Then we overschedule our kids in after-school and early-evening activities. Eager to support our children, we have come to believe that it is more important to watch a child's practice or game on the sidelines than to be home preparing a family meal. The result is that we eat in our cars or fast-food restaurants, or we bring home food to be consumed at a kitchen counter as kids drop by.

Then there is what happens when we do sit down to eat together. The majority of American families have the television on during dinner—a sure way to sap connecting talk out of the air. When we put little special thought into family dinner rituals (because we are so harried and distracted), the food and the conversation become boring and routine, and thus easy to skip. Children and adults alike are bombarded every day with rapid-fire commercials and MTV-like entertainment as we hurry through our schedules. How can family dinners compete?

There is another reason it is so hard to have good family meal rituals, something fundamental in our culture. We live in a highly individualistic age, and we are raising our children that way. We tend to see ourselves as providers of goods and services to our children, to keep them happy and satisfied. Eroding is the idea that children are citizens of families and communities, part of the whole, with obligations and responsibilities as contributing members to their family and community.

What does this have to do with family meals? We think that many parents see themselves as food providers rather than as leaders of a family dinner ritual. If you see the goal as simply to put food in the belly, then a family sit-down dinner is not necessary. Furthermore, if your goal is to please your children as customers, then you don't want to make them give up some other activity in order to eat with the family, or even to eat something they don't prefer to eat that day. The striking thing about family meals in an individualistic, consumerist culture is that they require social conformity: you have to gather at the same time; eat more or less the same food; make conversation together rather than read, play video games, or watch television; and finish at the same time. Sounds oppressive, doesn't it? McDonald's makes no such demands on its customers.

National Public Radio did a special on family dinners and their decline. The correspondent interviewed a sixteen-year-old girl about her family's dinner practices. She reported that her family rarely has dinner together, or any other meal for that matter. When asked why, she replied, without a trace of irony or negative emotion: "How can we be expected to eat together at the same time if we are not all hungry at the same time?" This is how the me-first, consumerist culture trumps family life. High-quality family dinners and other meals, where family members gather regularly for emotional and physical nourishment, are a countercultural practice in our contemporary world.

Finding the Time for Eating Together

For reclaiming family meals, our advice is simple but challenging.

- *Make family meals a priority.*
- *Be flexible.*
- *Start from where you are.*

Priority comes first. If you are having more than four family dinners together per week, you are probably already making a place for family meals in your life. By the way, you should count eating out together as a family dinner if you use the time for connection talk rather than just eating and running. See where your family stands by filling in the graph in Table 3.1, which can help you track who is at family meals for a week. If you can't do dinners together but have regular family breakfasts, weekend lunches, or brunches, then you are already ahead of many other families. But if you feel you do not have enough times when everyone in the family is together for a meal, then the first step is to diagnose the problem. Is it adult schedules or children's schedules? Too much individual pickiness about what people will eat? Fatigue or burnout in the chief cook? Have you drifted away from family meals for other reasons? The key is how badly you want to restore them. Only you can know that. The Graham family will have to start there: how badly do the parents want to restore their rich tradition of family dinners?

If you are sure you want to find time for family meals, then the next principle is to be flexible. In one busy family with four active children and a father who gets home late from work, the mother decided to feed the kids a snack early in the evening and have dinner at 8:00 P.M. every night. Everyone was home by then, no one had starved, and most of the busyness was over for the day. Another family is even more flexible. Here are the mother's words:

> We eat late—sometimes very late. We used to joke that we ate when one of my son's friends went to bed. At the time my son was nine years old and his friend went to bed at 8 P.M. Now, we joke that we eat when his friend's parents go to bed—sometimes as late as 10 P.M. My son is now seventeen years of age.
>
> Does the time of the meal matter? Not to me, as long as we all eat together. And with high-school activities planned all around the dinner hour, before and after, we don't squeeze the dinner hour to accommodate each person's schedule. The kids eat a mini-meal when they get home. But we eat dinner and relax around the dinner table and have even more things to share.
>
> Besides, one of the best pieces of advice my mom gave me is that it doesn't count when dinner is, just as long as it is before midnight.

You can also be flexible in your expectations for what you serve. If a family dinner means a five-course meal, then busy parents will throw in the dish towel pretty quickly and settle for take-home pizza in the living room in front of the television. The key is the conversation and the togetherness, not the menu.

TABLE 3.1

Who's Here?

Family Member	Sunday			Monday			Tuesday			Wednesday			Thursday			Friday			Saturday		
	B	L	D	B	L	D	B	L	D	B	L	D	B	L	D	B	L	D	B	L	D
NAME:																					

B = breakfast   L = lunch   D = dinner

Another way to be flexible is to add more cooks to the kitchen. In a family where Mom was getting pretty fried with cooking by herself, and tending to just have everyone reheat leftovers for themselves, the solution was to get Dad and the teenagers involved in owning certain meals during the week. Dad took Sunday nights and each teenager took one night during the week. The deal was that the cook also chose the menu, which meant that the nutritional pyramid (especially fruits, vegetables, and grains) wasn't adhered to every night. But more people involved in the chore part of meals meant the restoration of an important family ritual. A mother named Kathy likes to say that she gets very tired of running "Kathy's Country Kitchen," especially when the customers complain all the time. Kathy's family needs to absorb a core principle of family rituals: in general, the more people involved in putting on a ritual, the higher the quality of the ritual for everyone—and the more likely you are to do it regularly.

Our third piece of advice is to start from where you are. If one parent travels during the week, have dinner rituals with your children on weekdays and go all out on weekends when the whole family is present. Jo Ann, a single mother with a sixteen-year-old son who has a job and a car, became aware that she missed having dinners with him. Indeed, eating together at any time was a chance event. Sometimes she did not feel like she lived in a family with her son, since they had no regular contact. Jo Ann approached her son with the idea of setting aside one evening per week for a mother-son dinner. He was fine with the idea, and they decided to carve out Thursday evenings for their meal. They discussed in advance what to have, the son helped to prepare it, and they had a leisurely connecting dinner together.

Jo Ann had the good sense to start small, rather than propose eating together every night or telling her son to change his work schedule. And you can be sure that they both knew why they were there on Thursday nights. It was not just a feeding opportunity for two; it was a dinner ritual whose purpose was emotional connection between a mother and her son. Family meals tend to disappear gradually over time; they can be restored the same way, especially if they are made special in ways we will talk about next.

Making Meal Rituals Worth Having: Connection Talk

By this point, you might be saying to yourself: Give me a break! Have you been to my house recently for dinner? Togetherness? Conversation? How about boredom, complaining, and irritability? Indeed, there are good reasons besides crowded schedules why families drift away from family dinners and keep the television on when they do have them. As we mentioned before, we are a culture of speed and entertainment with a diminishing capacity for low-key hanging out together. A sense of emotional significance in family meals does not come automatically from sitting down at the same table together. We have to be intentional with our meal rituals in order to keep them fresh over the years. The box on page 37 has a number of questions you can ask yourself about what goes into the different phases of meal rituals in your family.

Since the heart of a meal ritual is conversation, let's start there. Logistics talk tends to take care of itself, with low-key conversation about who was involved in what activity that day, what is planned for tomorrow or next week, and announcements about being careful with the front step that is beginning to crack. The only problem with logistics talk is that if it dominates entirely, there is no room for connection talk.

Recall that connection talk mostly takes the form of stories, feelings, opinions, and humor. Some families we know are quite intentional about connection talk by beginning every meal with a "check-in": everyone mentions the best thing and the worst thing that happened to them that day. Even very young children can participate in this kind of connection ritual. The check-in can then be a springboard for further conversation about what is going on in everyone's lives.

The Crafting of Family Dinner Rituals: Questions to Ask Yourself

Advance Preparation Phase

- How are decisions made about which foods to purchase?
- How are predictability and novelty combined in purchasing food?
- How is food stored and made ready for meal preparation? It's harder to ritualize meals when no one has planned for what will be served.

Transition Phase: Getting Ready and Getting Seated

- Who prepares the meal, sets the table?
- Is the environment prepared for family time—TV off, newspapers removed, chairs arranged? Enhancements such as candles?
- When is the meal served?
- How are family members called to the table? Is there a struggle?
- Who is present? Do some come late? or not at all?

Enactment Phase: The Meal Itself

- Is the environment conducive to connection and conversation?
- How are family members seated?

- What kinds of food are served? How are family members' preferences balanced? Are there special foods sometimes?
- Are interruptions permitted, such as the phone?
- What topics of conversation are encouraged?
- What kinds of conversation are discouraged, e.g., discipline?

- Who participates in the conversations?
- How are table manners handled?

Exit Phase: Leaving the Table and Cleaning Up

- Is the end of the meal ritual clearly defined, with everyone leaving together?
- Who participates in cleanup?

Other families are less structured but nevertheless make efforts to have connecting talk during meals. When his children were growing up and paying more attention to the world around them, Bill liked to bring up events in the news. He would sometimes mention them to his wife and then ask the children if they had an opinion. For example, he might note that the new tobacco settlement banned outdoor cigarette advertising, which meant that the cartoon figure Joe Camel would be disappearing from public view. He would then ask the children if they were familiar with Joe Camel. Of course they were familiar with Joe Camel—all kids were, they replied. That gave him the opening to ask them what they thought about that advertisement, about smoking and its effects, about how many kids they knew at school who smoked, and about what effect they thought the ads had on kids. He would express his own opinions along the way, but the conversation was a give-and-take rather than an adult lecture about the evils of smoking.

Barbara remembers similar conversations with her four children about the unchaperoned spring break vacations that seniors at the local high school took every year to Cancun, Mexico. These annual opportunities for sex, drugs, and rock and roll were big news in the community. Long before her children were seniors, Barbara and her husband had dinnertime conversations concerning what they and the children thought about these events. As the kids got older, these conversations were opportunities to talk about what alcohol does to the judgment of young people—again, not a lecture, but a conversation in which the parents had the opportunity to listen and to share their values. By the way, none of Barbara's four children even asked to go to Cancun as seniors.

We don't mean to imply that most dinner conversations have to be about heavy topics. They can also be about baseball, the family dog, Grandma's health, parents' childhood memories, and who got scared by the thunder and lightning storm the night before. The key is that there is a chance for everyone to get involved in his or her own way. The box on page 40 gives you some fun conversation starters.

Connecting conversations can also go wrong. One mistake some parents make is to grill their children: What did you do today? What do you think of your math teacher? I saw your friend Lisa smoking outside the mall yesterday—were you aware she smokes? Especially as they approach adolescence, kids tend to hate feeling cross-examined by their parents, and will give one-word answers. It's generally a mistake to pursue them at these moments. An additional mistake is to make conversation-stopper comments when children open up. For example, when your twelve-year-old daughter says she hates math, a meal is not the time for admonishing her about her attitude or about how our society needs more women scientists. Another core principle of family rituals: minimal conflict. Almost every disciplinary matter, except kids hitting or throwing food at the table, can wait until after the meal ritual.

Conversation Starters for Mealtimes

- If you could go anywhere in the world, where would you go and why?
- Would you rather be a Jeep or a Porsche and why?
- Why doesn't glue stick to the inside of the bottle?
- What was your favorite family trip and why?
- What were the the worst thing and the best thing that happened today?
- If you were given $500 to do anything you want, what would you do?
- If you thought a stranger was following you, what would you do?
- If there were a fire in our home, what would you do?
- If you could meet any person in the world, who would it be and why?
- If you could meet someone from history, who would it be and why?
- Who is your favorite hero and why?
- What is your favorite television show and why?
- What is your all-time favorite movie and why?
- What do you value most about yourself? What would you like to improve on?
- Of what moment are you most proud?
- What was your most embarrassing moment?
- Would you rather have a party with a few friends or lots of friends?

- If you could have a whole day off from work or from school, what would you choose to do with that time?
- If our family wanted to do a service project together, what would you like to do?
- What is your most memorable first day of school?
- What happened during your favorite day at the beach?
- What is your favorite holiday and why?

Making Family Meals Worth Having: Being Creative

Okay, you say: I'm convinced that family meals (especially dinners) are important, that I should be flexible in setting them up, that I should start from where we are, and that I should be intentional about the conversations we have during meals. But where's the fun and the spontaneity? That's what we talk about now. But first, we want to stress that being creative does not mean that you become the entertainment director on the family cruise ship. Family meals are not a show that you put on for your family, followed by an applause meter or evaluation forms. There is great value in staying committed to regular family meals even when elements of boredom and fatigue set in. Family rituals, like the rest of life, have peaks and valleys, periods of intense enjoyment followed by periods where you look around the table and fantasize about being anywhere else than with this ungrateful, unruly batch of offspring and this detached or critical mate. But, as the saying goes, 80 percent of success in life comes from just showing up, whether you feel like it or not that day.

That said, we should put at least as much creative energy into our family meal rituals as we do into picking our wardrobes or enjoying our favorite hobby or planning a long-awaited vacation.

We put spices in our food, don't we? Why not put spice in our meal rituals? Here are some spice ideas we have gathered from our own experience and those of other families. More ideas can be found in the box below, "Tips for Family Fun."

Tips for Family Fun: Memorable Moments at Meals

Overall Meal Ideas

• Involve children in the meal, no matter their age—very young children can set the table, older children can cut vegetables and open cans, preteens and teens can be involved in the planning, shopping, cooking, and even be in charge of the entire meal. EVERYONE helps with the cleanup!

• Have a regular family night such as pizza night or taco night and watch your favorite family television show together. One family celebrates bread and soup night on Sundays. Dad bakes fresh bread, Mom prepares soup. The tantalizing aromas draw the family together to reconnect before the upcoming week.

• Buy a white tablecloth to use at each special holiday meal. Use permanent markers for family members to write or draw something that they are grateful for. Be sure to date the drawing and add a new thought every year. Each person could also have their own special birthday cloth to add to over the years.

• Have a special method to call the family to dinner: ring a bell, hit a gong, play a song on the piano, sing a gathering song.

• When children are grown and out of the house, create a Sunday family dinner—anyone who is in town is invited to gather. Don't forget grandparents.

• Keep a running list on the refrigerator door of topics to talk about at meals. Everyone adds to the list.

• Pray before every meal if that is part of your faith, and hold hands while you pray.

• Use your daily meal to celebrate EVERYTHING!—a good job in school, Mom or Dad's promotion, a clean bedroom, a lost tooth, every holiday from Arbor Day to Zeus Day.

Spice Up Your Meals

• When meals seem ho-hum, try eating in a different place—under the table, on a picnic blanket in front of the fireplace, in the tree house, in the yard, or at a park.

• Make your history come alive—study your heritage and find recipes from your ethnic background. Have the children do the research, help with the shopping, cook the meal, and make place mats, name cards, or a centerpiece that fits your country.

• Have a theme night. Go to the library and find books about many different countries, their culture and holidays. Prepare a meal from that culture and report on your research.

• Make mealtimes special with candles, the good dishes, and a tablecloth. Eat in the dining room.

• Find a book that teaches about the food pyramid and have the family work hard to follow it.

• Occasionally change places at the table and let everyone have a chance to be at the head.

• Go on a $2.00 date. Everyone gets $2.00 to find the best dinner value.

Food Ideas

• Make s'mores (a roasted marshmallow and a piece of chocolate squished between two graham crackers) in the fireplace or the microwave.

• Take a "field trip" and create something delicious with your bounty: applesauce or apple pie from the trip to the apple orchard, jam from the strawberry farm, baked seeds from the pumpkin patch.

• End the meal with a dessert project. Frost cupcakes, decorate cookies, make ice cream or sundaes, and then eat them.

For Young Children

• Take the children with you when you do the grocery shopping and let them each choose an item.

• Paint secret messages on a piece of bread with milk mixed with food coloring. Toast the bread and the message magically appears.

• Have an all-one-color meal. Everything must be green or red, etc. Get creative!

• Have an alphabet meal. Choose one letter and have all food items begin with that letter—for example, peanut butter sandwiches, purple juice, plums, popcorn, pretzels, pears, pigs in a blanket.

• Read Dr. Seuss's book *Green Eggs and Ham* and then make them for dinner.

• Modify the environment. The Dohertys like to light a candle, lower the lights with a dimmer switch, and put on soft music in the background. This creates "ritual space," where family members enter a different mood than they had been in before. The effect is to soothe the hyper beast in all of us.

• Barbara sometimes would announce that the Carlson dinner that night would be held under the table! All hands belowdecks! Other times dinner might be in the tree house, in the yard, or at the beach.

• If you live in a cold climate where you cannot picnic during the winter, have a picnic on a blanket in front of the fireplace. Barbara did that with her family when she thought a change of scenery was in order. It's fun to roast marshmallows on an indoor fire.

• Make one dinner a week really special. Here is the story from the Kakuk family, told in the mother's (Sue's) words:

I don't cook on Thursday nights! While we typically shared all our evening meals together, they seemed like a chore and uneventful. Last New Year's, I got organized and finally cleaned off the dining room table for a special family dinner that we planned for just the four of us. We hadn't eaten in there in over ONE year! While the meal itself wasn't particularly special, we dressed the table with a festive tablecloth, napkins, napkin rings, candles, good china and glassware, etc. We enjoyed it so much, I suggested we eat in there once a week. Then to my surprise, my husband suggested that he and the kids take turns preparing the meal. What a deal! Each week, they plan their menu and I grocery shop for it. Sometimes it's mac 'n' cheese or chicken noodle soup. Who cares? But we still eat it in the dining room with the good china. . . . We are proud to see our kids take some control and gain confidence in the kitchen.

• Have the kids make place mats for the table.

• Have a breakfast meal for dinner. When Bill was out of town, his wife would sometimes prepare Danish pancakes for dinner for herself and the children. Novel food tends to create a fun mood.

• Go all-out when you eat take-home food. One family sometimes does the tablecloth, the good dishes, candles—the whole works—when they do take-home Chinese out of cardboard containers.

• Take advantage of weekend brunch opportunities for playful meal rituals. One father remembers with fondness how his own father used to take special orders for pancakes on Sunday mornings, each in the form of a cartoon character of a child's choice—Mickey Mouse, Donald Duck, you name it—and Dad would make them. When the grown-up children return home with their own children, what do you think they ask for on Sunday mornings?

We are inspired with the stories we hear from families who use their creativity and persistence to make dinners and other meals the cornerstone of their family time together. We understand the powerful forces that keep many families from breaking bread together. But we believe deeply that for most families, the first beachhead in the battle to reclaim family life is their meal rituals. Make your stand here if you can. Be committed and flexible, accept where you are starting from, develop your skills in family conversation, realize that there will be dry times, and have some creative fun along the journey. In this way, you will pass along an important family tradition to your children that will carry on when they have families. As we know from our own personal experience, your children will be grown up before you turn around twice, and you will be thankful that you nurtured and preserved your family culture by dedication to your meal rituals.

· 4 ·

Now I Lay Me Down to Sleep:
Reclaiming Bedtime

W hat comes into your mind when you think of childhood and bedtime? Do you have warm, cozy feelings? Memories of arguments and power struggles? A combination of both? Bedtime can be the best and worst time in everyday family life, best when it brings intimate connection between parents and children, worst when it ends a tiring day with an even more tiring battle of wills.

Bedtime rituals are a modern thing. Throughout most of history, families went to bed when the sun went down and arose when it came up the next morning. They did not have lightbulbs to extend daylight and create choices about when to end their day's activities. For the most part, families lived in small dwellings without separate quarters for their many children to have private chats with parents at night. Bedtime as a special ritual probably did not enter the picture until the twentieth century, and may not have become commonplace until the second half of the century. The following scenario described by Taffy marks her as a modern mother using a bedtime ritual to create intimate moments with her daughter.

My daughter, now four, likes to tell me a story at bedtime. Then I tell her a story. She usually asks me for ideas for her stories. I have to give a few before we hit on one she likes. But then I love to hear her tell her tale. It helps me to know what's on her mind.

Like Taffy, most of us know that we hear things from our children during bedtime rituals that we do not hear any other way. The pressures and busyness of the day are now over, and in a warm, quiet bedroom environment, or cuddled up on the living room sofa, we experience a special kind of emotional connection with our children. Not every time, of course. The power of ritual is not that every occasion is deep or memorable, but that our faithfulness to it creates possibilities for deep, memorable connections over time.

The Current Threat to Bedtime Rituals

Researchers are beginning to document what many of us are seeing: bedtime rituals are now in decline. Kids nowadays are less apt to have regular times to go to bed, and without this structure, it is difficult to have bedtime rituals. Instead, children are staying up—watching television, exchanging instant messages, playing video games, or doing homework—until they decide they are ready for bed. A lot of young children fall asleep somewhere in the house and are carried to bed by a parent. At that point, a bedtime ritual involving talking, storytelling, or reading is not in the cards.

Even federal health officials are becoming worried. The National Heart, Lung, and Blood Institute is starting a campaign to encourage better sleep habits among children. Too many children, the Institute says, do not get enough sleep, and the result is problems such as difficulties with schoolwork and relationships with friends and family.

What is going on here? Why are we slipping backward on a unique and important family ritual that helps with both sleep and family bonding? The reasons go to the heart of our message in this book.

• *Frantic family schedules.* Kids who are charging around from the time school lets out until nighttime are often too wired to settle into a bedtime ritual with a parent. And the parents are too frazzled to enter into the slowing-down process of a full bedtime ritual.

• *Television.* Left to their own devices, most children would rather watch one more TV show than go to bed. And they may fall asleep in front of the TV. No chance then for a bedtime ritual.

• *The Internet.* At least television tends to make a tired watcher think about sleep. But interactive chat rooms and instant messaging are engaging and awakening, which can make it harder to wind down toward bedtime.

• *Homework.* Children today have more homework than children of previous generations. Combined with extracurricular activities, homework pushes the evening hours later and later.

• *Working parents.* Some working parents tell us that they miss spending more time with their children, and therefore keep them up later at night to spend time together. They may feel guilty about banishing their kids to bed before they want to go to sleep. Unfortunately, parents are missing one of the most important ways they can connect with their children.

• *Tired parents.* Let's face it: most of us are tired by the end of the day, even if we are not overscheduled. It takes extra effort to read, talk, sing songs, or tell stories to a child at a time when our body and mind are saying, "Enough!"

• *Wimpy parents.* This goes back to the lack of structured bedtimes. Most kids will not voluntarily sign up for a regular bedtime, and without a regular bedtime it's hard to have a ritual. To make bedtime rituals work, parents have to impose an orderly bedtime on their children, an exercise of consistent authority that many contemporary parents find difficult. Ironically, when you exercise confident authority in this area, children tend to cooperate on their own, and even like it, so that bedtimes do not seem like a power move by parents.

When It's Bad, It's Dreadful!

Bobby's parents did not have a problem of having an overscheduled family, but they exemplify the problem of insecure parents not being able to make a bedtime stick. They had never really established a routine bedtime for their five-year-old son, letting him stay up as a toddler and preschooler until he got sleepy and wanted to go to bed. Now that Bobby is starting a morning kindergarten schedule, his parents wanted to create a bedtime routine. Previously, they would sometimes read to him in the evening on the living room sofa, but now they wanted to have a real bedtime with talks and reading in bed. Plus they wanted Bobby to get enough sleep for kindergarten.

Bobby would have none of it. An effective bargainer at age five, he believed he had a constitutional right to stay up until he decided to go to bed. After all, he knew nothing else in his young life. He negotiated every night. Sometimes it was about finishing a favorite video. Other times it was about continuing to play with his toys or a video game. He whined that he was not tired. He had angry outbursts and refused to brush his teeth and get into his pajamas. By the time his mother got him into bed, neither of them was in a mood for a story or a quiet talk. When finally put to bed, he would often leave his room and beg for a snack or a glass of milk. The whole scene could go on for hours.

Bobby's mother was more insistent on establishing a bedtime than his father was—and Bobby knew it. He would wheedle more time out of this father, who was rarely the "bad guy" to do the nasty deed of getting Bobby to bed. When Mom was not available in the evening, Dad did not enforce bedtime. When Bobby came out of his room to ask for a treat, Dad would give it to him if Mom was not around to say no. You can imagine how frustrated Mom was getting.

It's not that Bobby's dad was an uncaring father. It's just that he was a "pacifist parent," a father who did not want to be authoritarian like his own father. He saw little point to ending the day with a power struggle that upset everyone. Eventually the mother gave up trying to establish a regular bedtime for Bobby, thus eliminating the possibility of an enriching bedtime ritual. You see, it's knowing that bedtime is coming, just as surely as the sun sets in the west, that motivates children to want to make the best of it by connecting with their parents. Left to their own devices, most children would decide each day whether they wanted to stay up and do their own thing or go to bed and spend special time with their parents. And if they get to decide each day, then they will resent parents' efforts to create a regular structure. Negative negotiations and conflict will ensue each night, and the possibility of a meaningful bedtime ritual will go away. You've got to be in charge to make family time work for you and your children.

When It's Good, It's Very, Very Good

There are lots of ways to make bedtime rituals a highlight of your family life. We want to tell you how we did them with our kids, and how some other families do it. In Barbara's family, bedtime began with "Last one up is a rotten egg!" There was a mad rush up the stairs where the four children and two parents fell into a giggling heap at the top of the stairs. Cuddling close, each person, adults and children alike, shared one good thing that happened that day, and one bad thing. (Barbara loved this way to check in with each child; they often shared the "bad" things at bedtime that they had not shared earlier.) They would then sing a song for each child, composed specially for each child by their father, Sam. Next was a simple prayer and a request for blessings for specific family members and friends. And they would end by reading a book and tucking each child into bed. It was a fulsome ritual that put a capstone on the day.

In Bill's family, he was in charge of the bedtime ritual, which was one to one with each child. His wife was glad to have a break from the kids, and Bill liked the one-to-one time with each child. There was a set bedtime that gradually became later as the children got older. When the children were young, bedtime would start with baths at 7:30 P.M., followed by pajamas and a good night kiss from their mother. The bedroom talk always started with Eric, the oldest, but Elizabeth would sometimes watch the time her father spent with Eric, in order to make sure she got equal time! Sometimes Bill would read a story, but mostly he and each child just talked or goofed around by playing hide-and-seek under the covers or singing silly songs. He remembers Eric at a certain age being afraid of burglars, and pretending that Dad was a burglar to be pounded on (a more active exercise than normally recommended for bedtime). With Elizabeth, who could at times be an oppositional child, he remembers playfully singing together the Beatles song "Hello, Goodbye." Sometimes the children talked about what was troubling them, and sometimes the discussions were about religion or the big bang theory and the origin of the universe. These bedtime talks were the high point of the day in the Doherty household.

Notice that both families' bedtime rituals were regular and predictable. Of course there were conflicts and struggles sometimes, but by and large they were peaceful. As parents, we never used these occasions for disciplinary talks, and the children learned to go with the flow rather than ask for special privileges that they knew would not be granted (such as extra food or leaving the room). The following are more bedtime ritual stories, told in the words of the parents themselves. The first one is from Sally.

> The secret to our bedtime success was really simple. From the time the boys were infants, we'd bathe them around seven P.M., and give them that before-bed feeding. As they grew older, it turned into a bath plus books (whatever timed out to about twenty to thirty minutes of reading). We kept it simple and consistent. We have always had a bedtime, and we have almost always (except on vacations) held consistent to it. The boys don't seem to mind at all. In fact, now that my oldest is going on fifteen, he appreciates a reasonable bedtime, and will often head to bed at the same time every evening on his own steam. My youngest (twelve) still has a set bedtime, and I think he sees it as a kind of sanctuary, a set time he can just relax and read. We've talked about reinstating reading aloud for his bedtime . . . not sure if we'll read to him or he'll read to us . . . but I thought we'd start it back up this fall.

Notice the power of "simple and consistent," and also how the family has adapted as the children got older. Regularity and flexibility—those are the hallmarks of a family that uses its time well. The next story is from Lori, who also talks of consistency and adds the idea of preventing the common problem of overtired kids.

> We too have had a simple bedtime routine. We usually start an hour before actual bedtime (barring special visitors, occasions, or vacation). We do baths, watch some of their favorite

shows together (especially *Arthur*), have a small snack at the coffee table, and then read on the couch for the last half hour. The most important part is being together quietly for a period of time before they go to bed. With summertime, bedtime is later and we usually end up with not as much time (we never want to come in from outside), but we still do baths, snack, and reading to keep things consistent. They have always gone right to bed and to sleep. Nightmares have never been a problem either, and I like to think it's because we've been so careful to keep things consistent right before bed. I know I could count on one hand the amount of times we've let them get overtired. I think that's important too.

Lori adjusts the time and duration of the bedtime ritual to the summer hours, but maintains its basic structure. Next, Nancy describes the power of bedtime stories for young children.

My daughters are twenty and seventeen and we have always had bedtime routines. When they were younger it was baths, snacks, books, and being tucked in. I started at least an hour before bedtime when they were toddlers because they loved to play in the bathtub. As they got older and took care of bathing themselves, I still tried to be nearby, putting away laundry and tidying bedrooms to keep them on track. We went to the library frequently and always had a lot of new picture books to read as well as old favorites. As they got older, we graduated to chapter books, even though they could both read already. One of their favorite family stories is when we read the last chapter of *Where the Red Fern Grows.* I was crying as I read the last chapter of the story and the two of them started sobbing. Their dad yelled up from the first floor: "WHAT is going on up there?" "Oh, Daddy, this story is soooo good." One of my best "mother" moments was when my older daughter told me that when she reads to herself she "hears" my voice. Isn't that the coolest thing?

Indeed, this is one of the coolest things a parent could hear. So often the parent voices in our heads are the reminding, nagging, reprimanding ones. Nancy's daughter carries her mother's soft, hypnotic reading voice. Nancy goes on to talk about the importance of tucking in older children.

As they got older and busier, we discontinued reading aloud, but I continued to tuck them in, which involved fixing covers, a kiss good night, and the rhyme:

Good night sleep tight,
see you in the morning light
I love you sweet potato.

When they were small they would request other vegetables, such as "I love you my little head of cabbage" or "my little plum tomato." We had a German exchange student living with us for a year and she loved the whole tucking-in routine. (She always just said good night to her mother and went to bed.) Every night I would hear her lilting German accent saying, "Nancy, I'm ready to be tucked in now." The tucking in gives kids an opportunity to talk about what is on their minds, to talk about little hurts that happened during the day at school or between us. I should have planned more time for the tucking in as they became teenagers, because we often stayed up too late talking. I think the bedtime routine helped me get through the teenage years as much as it did the toddler years.

Next we hear from Sue, describing how she and her husband reclaimed a bedtime ritual when their daughter became a teenager. She also notes what is missing when they skip the ritual.

> When the kids were younger, my husband would read to one child in their bed, while I read to the other. As my daughter got older, she really wanted to read her own books to herself, so we simply stopped spending that time with her. We lost something! My son is now ten and will do everything to be ready at bedtime so that we can read that next chapter and spend time together. As for my daughter, now thirteen, we may not read to her anymore, but we stretch out in bed next to her with our own book. We have some good quiet time together, she doesn't feel left out, and we usually end up talking about something. If we've had too busy an evening and send them to bed with just hugs and kisses, they are always getting out of bed to tell us something.

There are lots of good material here for understanding bedtime rituals and child development. Notice how Sue's son, at age ten, looks forward to the next chapter of a gripping story, along with the emotional connection that comes with it. For their thirteen-year-old daughter, Sue and her husband were creative in finding a new bedtime ritual. Reading in bed beside the daughter allows closeness but freedom to talk or not talk. With that freedom granted, she usually talks. And Sue notices what happens when the evening ends without the bedtime ritual. There is unfinished business from the day, unprocessed stress that comes out in other ways.

Finding Time for Bedtime Rituals

Let's pull together the take-to-bed messages we want to pass on about bedtime rituals. ("Tips for Fun and Restful Family Bedtime Rituals" can be found in the box on page 60.)

• *Create a regular bedtime hour and stick to it.* Don't argue about it every night. Make it an inevitable part of your child's life and your family's evening routine. If you have not created a routine bedtime yet, then call a family meeting to talk about it, giving your explanations and setting up the plan. And stay with the plan long enough to make it work, having further family meetings if necessary to reinforce your intention to persist. Congratulate your reluctant children the next morning if they cooperated the night before. Once you establish the routine, even if it's difficult, the payoff will start to occur in doing this connecting ritual. But you have to persevere.

• *Spend at least thirty minutes winding down before bedtime.* This can be with a bath, a snack, or quiet time. Let your children know in advance that it will soon be time to start the bedtime preparation, rather than springing it on them suddenly when they are in the middle of some other activity. For example: "Jonathon, remember that in a little while we will have to start getting ready for bed."

• *Think slow.* Bedtime rituals are a slow-down time in a speeded-up world. Allow enough time to go through the routine at a leisurely pace.

• *Involve your child in choosing the connecting activities that make ritual special:* books to read, what things to talk about, what other quiet activities to do.

• *Avoid bringing up disciplinary matters.* Don't even bring up logistical matters such as the car-pool schedule. Leave those issues for another time. In the same way, teach your children to respect the ritual time by not bringing up requests for consumer purchases or permissions to do special activities. Just tell them that those matters can wait until tomorrow because right now you are doing bedtime things. Respect rituals as time freed from everyday business and busyness.

• *Make the ritual long enough for pleasurable and meaningful contact with your child.* But keep it short enough that you can manage it along with your own responsibilities in the evening.

• *Once you have kissed your children good night, do not permit them to leave the bedroom unless something is clearly wrong.* Make sure they have used the bathroom already. No more snacks. No questions than can wait until tomorrow. If your children leave the bedroom, quietly but firmly put them back in bed. No yelling on your part, which will just get the children worked up and give them unnecessary and negative attention.

• *Do not insist that your child fall asleep right away.* Falling asleep is an involuntary thing, and you will not win that power struggle. You can insist that your child stay in bed with lights out. In the case of Bill's son, Eric, who did not need a lot of sleep, he was allowed to play quietly in his room until he felt ready for sleep.

• *In a two-parent family, consistency is the name of the game.* Make sure that both of you are on board with the bedtime rules. Likewise, both parents should be interchangeable in being able to carry out the bedtime ritual. It's a mistake to have one parent be the only one who can manage bedtime. The other parent (often Dad) loses out on intimate connection with the children, and the family schedule is thrown off if the key parent is not available.

• *In a single-parent family, it's also about consistency.* We know it's hard to find the energy to do bedtime rituals every night. But the payoff for tomorrow and the future makes this investment worth it. You feed them every night no matter how you feel. Do the same with bedtime rituals if at all possible.

• *A stepparent should go easy on enforcing bedtime.* See if you can slowly follow your spouse's lead during bedtime rituals. Sit around and listen during book reading, then offer to share the reading. Follow the children's lead and comfort level, but try to work your way into bedtime rituals over time. It will help you bond with them and add cohesion to the whole family.

• *If you must be out of town regularly, consider a scheduled phone call at bedtime to connect with your child.* You can review the good and bad things that happened that day. The same thing goes for a nonresidential parent, who can call the children at bedtime if there is an agreement about this with the residential parent.

• *Be creative.* Except for the general principles of consistency and connection, there are no fixed rules for how to do bedtime rituals. Notice how our own bedtime rituals—Barbara's and Bill's— were so different, and yet they worked beautifully in our families.

In this book, we have focused first on meals and bedtimes because these are the everyday ingredients of family life. We have to eat more than once a day, and we have to sleep every day. Family life is all about these daily rhythms that we share with other mammals and their young. There is no more powerful ritual in family life than exchanging the last words of the day, the last kiss, the last "I love you," the final tucking-in as the sun disappears and we enter the world of sleep and dreams.

Tips for Fun and Restful Family Bedtime Rituals

- Try to have a bedtime talk with each child or as the whole family.
- Say prayers every night if that is part of your faith.
- A favorite stuffed toy or blanket gives children a feeling of security. One high-school student shared the fact that Winnie the Pooh will be going to college with her.
- Have a family teeth-brushing event each night.
- Read a favorite book before bed.
- With older children, read a chapter of a special book each night. They will be eager to see what happens next.
- Have a ritual snack before bed (warm milk with marshmallows, hot chocolate, animal crackers, etc.).
- Bath time can be creative with soap crayons and floating toys that can only be used during evening baths.
- Take time to brush your daughter's hair.
- Make your rocking chair the bedtime throne and sing songs together.
- Let each child ask for their favorite song.
- Try different ways to kiss good night. For example, rub noses for an Eskimo kiss, flutter your eyelashes on your child's cheek for a butterfly kiss, hum the Batman tune as you come in for a Batman kiss, or give a very demonstrative kiss for a dinosaur kiss.
- If you can't be home at bedtime, call and send a tele-hug to each child.

But It's Not on the Schedule!
Reclaiming Time to Just Hang Out

Earlier we told the story of the six-year-old girl who cried while waiting for her mother to pick her up at school. The girl longed just to be at home, but instead she was facing a marathon of automobile drives and activities, not only her own but those of her siblings. You see, even if each individual child is not overscheduled, the sum total of scheduled activities may put everyone on tilt. Little ones cannot stay home, so they have to travel around to their siblings' events. Each additional sibling adds exponentially to the stress. Today's families, suffering from time famine, lack opportunities to "hang out" at home and in their neighborhood.

For those of us raised in the pre–daily planner era, hanging out had a mixed reputation as a childhood activity. We all knew kids who were not active enough in sports and play, who watched too much television, who did little except to hang out, especially in the summer. Hanging out on a street corner suggested that a group of teenagers was not productively engaged and might get into trouble. Nowadays it's tempting for teens to watch MTV for hour upon hour, or interact with others mainly on the Internet, and not be involved enough in school and other community activities.

Over the past fifteen years or so, the word has gotten out to parents and community leaders that children and youth need to do something other than hang out. They need stimulating, structured activities that involve them with other young people and with caring adults in the community. There is good research to support the wisdom of this idea. But the problem is that many of us have taken the message too far: if a moderate amount of structured activities is good for kids, then more must be better. Let's keep them super busy so that they do not get into trouble.

Have no doubt: there still are children and teens who are not involved enough in structured activities outside the home, who miss out on the enrichment that school, faith community, and other community organizations can offer. On the other hand, typically these are kids who do not have a rich home life either. The kids who are in trouble with too much time on their hands are the ones who spend too little time with their parents and siblings, not just too little time in structured activities. A rich family life and a rich community life go hand in hand. The challenge is to find the balance, and in the current generation of parents, the more neglected side is the family, hands down.

The Lost Art of Hanging Out as a Family

By hanging out, we mean being around home without a schedule. Many of us remember this as the foundation of our childhood. On a weekend or summer day, we would figure out what to do alone or with our siblings, friends, and parents. We had toys, books, games, and sports to choose from. We had to develop the skill of attracting other kids to play what we wanted to play, or making sure we had a stock of library books to read on a rainy summer afternoon. For Bill's family, Sundays were generally times to hang out as a family, with church in the morning and being around in the afternoon and evening. He remembers the newspaper comic strips, the Philadelphia Phillies baseball games on television (or at the ballpark itself), and sometimes a Sunday drive or a visit to relatives. School nights involved a combination of homework and just being around (with very little weekday television) until bedtime. Special treats were when we played family games such as Sorry. Other than these times for hanging out with family, Bill's nonschool days were filled with intense play with his friends on Belmar Street in Philadelphia, out of sight and sound of his parents.

In Barbara's family, the best hanging-out time was spent "up north." In Minnesota, many families have cabins in the northern part of the state where they enjoy life on the edge of one of Minnesota's fifteen thousand lakes. Summertime meant weekends and several weeks at the cabin filled with spontaneous, unstructured family time. The cabin had no phone or television, water came from the lake, and the "powder room" was at the end of a dirt path. Barbara and her siblings spent hours playing in the water, visiting grandparents two doors down, chasing frogs, reading, and fishing. The day revolved around long leisurely meals, often shared with aunts, uncles, cousins, and grandparents.

In today's highly scheduled families, many children and parents seem to be losing their ability to hang out together. Unaccustomed to entertaining themselves, kids complain of being bored, and parents feel responsible for entertaining them. The kids reject the recommendations of their "recreation director" parents, get antsy and irritable, and throw themselves into mindless television watching or Web surfing. (Some educators complain that modern television has raised young children's expectations for entertainment with the constant change of attention-getting material.)

The parents, hating to see their children in a funk, resolve to keep them busier in the future.

Of course, we adults are part of this problem, too. Studies show that the majority of American adults who are raising children feel rushed much of the time. Nearly every invention that saves us time eventually costs time. Take the automobile: we travel much more quickly than in the horse-and-buggy days, but then we book ourselves all over town and have less time to hang out with our family. Airplanes get us places incredibly fast, but then we spend more time away from home. A cellular phone means that we can coordinate our schedules to the minute. E-mail has allowed work to invade our home lives.

If we are not careful, we will lose our capacity to simply be at home with our families. As in rarely using a muscle, we will lose our imagination about what we might do with our children, and what they might do on their own. Our children will lose the special creativity born out of lots of time to dream, imagine, and invent things to do. And they will grow up without even nostalgic memories of times that were slow enough to enjoy their families and their neighborhood.

Being Around Without a Schedule

What's so important about hanging out together as a family? What it gives is the chance for spontaneous connection. You may be doing things in different rooms in the house, and then your child wanders into the kitchen or garage where you are casually doing a chore or working on a hobby. The two of you might pick up a conversation as your child watches you work, or you might invite the child to join in the cookie baking or the woodcutting. We all know how important these moments can be. If you are too rushed, or if your child is hurrying to get ready for the next scheduled event, then these spontaneous connections don't happen.

Time to hang out can lead to play. It might be a board game or playing catch, either of which comes with a sense of freedom from a schedule. Games have the unique ingredient of putting parents and children on the same level for a time, cooperating or playfully competing as equals. Points scored against parents are a source of glee for a child who is so often on the lower end of the authority scale. Parents can let their hair down and be silly, make mistakes, or even pretend to compete fiercely. None of this happens with a sense of time urgency. You don't say, "Get the Monopoly game out and set it up quickly; we're on a tight schedule!"

Hanging out as a family also means that children have to learn to relate to their siblings. Most structured community activities are set up by age group, but living in a family generally means dealing with siblings (and cousins) who are not your age and don't necessarily share your exact interests and abilities. Siblings left alone to hang out together are forced to entertain one another. Older ones teach things to younger ones; younger ones cajole older ones into activities that are "beneath" their status. Siblings have to resolve differences. Of course, this means more potential for sibling conflict and stress on parents. But the long-term payoffs for the relationships between siblings are worth the challenge.

Time to hang out brings the opportunity for play with neighborhood children. The absence of kids to play with spontaneously is one of the sad outcomes of overscheduling children in structured activities. There is no one to play with in the afternoons, early evenings, weekends, or summers in many neighborhoods. This forces many parents to overschedule their own children so that they can be with other kids. But if a group of parents decides to have more unscheduled time, children will find one another and experience the kind of creative play activities that only come about when kids have time on their hands and imaginations to fill it. Bugs Peterschmidt tells the story of the neighborhood children gathering to jump into and bury themselves in the piles of fall leaves. Some children still sell lemonade at sidewalk stands during hot summer afternoons. These are child-generated activities, with minimal adult supervision, that only happen when families allow time for their children to hang out at home.

Time to hang out also provides opportunities for kids to share some of the family responsibilities. Many families purposefully turn chores into fun and games. One summer Barbara was frustrated with the seemingly endless amount of housework and yard work and her children's dawdling to get their chores done. One morning the kids were abruptly awakened by reveille and soon faced their mother, whistle in hand, welcoming them to Camp Carlson! A large duty board presented itself with the promise that as soon as all the chores were done, a fun activity of their choice would fill the afternoon. The children enjoyed racing each other as they did their chores and the family got a clean house with no whining. Afternoons were spent at the beach, at the zoo, and in the park. Barbara never knew what an impact this activity had on her kids until many years later when her grown children confided that they had proudly shared Camp Carlson in their college child development and education classes.

Finally, time to hang out means being available for company and for visiting relatives and friends. There was an era not long ago when families spontaneously visited one another in the evening and on weekends. The assumption was that most people were at home and would welcome company. Before telephones, there was little alternative to dropping by, and even after telephones, it was not considered necessary, in many communities, to call in advance of a visit. Those days are now gone; today's manners advisers insist that we call ahead first. But nowadays most of us don't even think about calling to ask another family if we can drop by, or if they would like to come to visit, because we assume they will be too busy. (We are also more privacy-oriented than any generation in history.) Our point is that time to hang out as a family, if we know other families who are doing the same, allows for possibilities of community connections that do not have to be booked weeks in advance. In the story that follows, note that the family reaped benefits both for themselves and for their relationship with another family after making the decision to have more time to hang out one summer.

Claire and her family decided to take a summer off from outside activities to see what it was like to hang out as a family. It had been after many years of sports, Scouts, and other activities. Their twelve-year-old daughter, a gifted gymnast, was particularly busy all year. Why a summer sabbatical? Claire and her husband had gotten involved in conversations in their community about the problem of overscheduled kids and underconnected families. They then listened more closely to their daughter, who sometimes mentioned that she missed having dinners with the family because of her gymnastics practices. With another frantic summer approaching, Claire and her husband decided to try something radical: a summer with no outside activities other than synagogue and necessary childcare.

The result was enlightening. For the first time since Claire could remember, the family had dinner together every night, ending with a conversation about what they might do that evening. They made it up as they went along, sometimes going for walks, sometimes playing games, sometimes doing solo activities. There was an even more surprising development. A member of a family they were close to had a serious health problem, and Claire, her husband, and her children were able to spend many evenings over at their friends' house, the parents talking with the adults and the children playing together. Claire mentioned that this kind of family-to-family connection would have been unthinkable during a normal summer schedule. When the fall came, the family talked about their year's schedule. The children did get reinvolved in some of their favorite activities, but with less intensity and more opportunity for dinners and hanging out as a family.

Hanging Out with a Purpose

So far we've talked about hanging out as creating the unstructured space for something good to happen in the family. Some families also develop regular rituals for using this time carved out from busy family schedules. Here are a couple of examples, first from Sue and then from Leslie. We told Sue's story about having a family-cooked meal on Thursday nights. Here is the follow-up ritual that emerged from dinner.

> We follow the meal with a game or reading a chapter from a book. If the kids get invites on Thursday evening, they proudly decline, explaining it is our family night. We all look forward to the "event" and, as parents, the attitudes and evening conversations are unforgettable!

Leslie's family has an extended ritual for their Monday nights at home, one that is supported by their religious community. Notice also that everyone is involved.

> We also like the idea of having "family nights" set aside for bonding family activities and discussions. We have had family home evenings for years on Monday nights. Some have been successes and some have not. Sticking with the habit has been the key. Our family nights are Scripture/

values based but range all over the place as far as interest or topic. We have always had a "Family Home Evening" assignment board that rotates responsibilities for each family member each week (lesson, song, prayer, activity, and treats are the responsibilities that rotate each week). We have had family home evenings that focus on organization/cleanliness, when we talked about the value of the time we have each been given and how organization helps conserve and use that time wisely. We have had a family room cleanup, yard cleanup activity and have shared ideas on bedroom organization, etc. We have played various styles of music, asked which the family members liked best, constructed cheap instruments from household items, composed a family song or cheer and performed it.

What families do with the hanging-out time must change as children get older and their interests and abilities change. That's the tricky part of all family rituals: just when you have it down, things change. Bill and his wife and children used to watch Alfred Hitchcock movies on Friday nights. It was a lovely way to hang out together. But after exhausting all of Hitchcock's movies, we had to move on to other ways to be together, because we could find no other filmmaker we all liked!

Finding Time to Hang Out Well

When talking about slowed-down family time, we run the risk of sounding nostalgic for long-ago days that will never return. In this era of two-earner families and single-parent families and many more opportunities for children, most families will not be able to just hang out together for long stretches of days. Life is more complex. But we believe that it is possible for many families to reclaim enough hanging-out time to enrich their lives. Here are strategies we have learned from families who have successfully done it. Look at the box at the end of this chapter for lots of specific ideas for having a fun time hanging out as a family.

- *Schedule time to hang out.* This may sound like a contradiction, but it's not. If you don't carve out unscheduled time on your calendar, it won't happen. You have to be intentional about it. One family decided that Sundays, aside from religious activities, would have no schedule. The parents informed the coaches of this decision and stuck by it. The children were baffled at first, but just as with bedtimes, if the children know that a certain day is for family time, like it or not, then they tend to get creative about making the best of it.
- *Be open to having "nothing" happen during hanging-out time.* In other words, don't build in high expectations, especially at the beginning. Your family will find its own way.
- *Look for spontaneous things to do together.* One of Barbara's fondest memories is a hot summer day when she went outside and her son playfully turned the hose on her. Feeling particularly spontaneous, Barbara went into the house and came out armed with a water pistol. A raucous water fight soon erupted and quickly involved the entire family. From then on, Barbara packed water pistols in the closet for impromptu fun.
- *Think about possible things to do while hanging out,* especially if you anticipate a long stretch of time. Before a summer with no outside activities, Bugs worked with her children to develop a list of over one hundred activities they could do in the summer if they got bored. These involved work around the house, new skills to learn, and other, simpler things to do.

• *Be creative, but don't feel like the recreation director on a cruise ship.* Your family may have a "shake down" period before settling into a pattern of using hanging-out time well. Don't let the b-word ("bored") shake your confidence. No one ever died of boredom.

• *If regular rituals evolve, let them happen,* and check with family members if they want to keep doing them. Remember Sue, who moved one New Year's dinner into the dining room with the nice dishes? It was a big hit and turned into a weekly ritual that eventually evolved to include playing a game after dinner.

• *Don't let television or the Internet fill all the available space you've freed up* on your family schedule. See chapter 7.

• *Use small moments to connect.* A pat on the back, a surprise kiss, or a spontaneous waltz around the room only takes a moment but is a sure means of connection.

Hanging out as a family is a countercultural act in today's world. It serves no competitive purpose. You don't pay for it. You usually can't point to something notable that anyone in the family learned or accomplished. You can't easily brag about it to friends. There is no scorecard or win-loss record, no coach or teacher, no competency levels, no easily identifiable skills, no entry on a college résumé. Sometimes it's boring, sometimes siblings will fight the whole time, and your e-mails are piling up silently somewhere on a server. But does anyone doubt that we must, for the sake of our children and our communities, reclaim and restore the time to hang out together with those we love most on the planet? Now put this book down and hang out with someone in your family.

Tips for Family Fun:
Ideas for Hanging Out

Anytime Fun

• Learn about your heritage. Put on a play, make a meal, do a craft from your culture of origin.

• Bring out home videos and picture albums and share old times.

• Turn on the radio or CD player and all join in some interpretive dancing.

• Turn ordinary trips to the dentist or doctor into a one-on-one celebration with a stop at the ice-cream store or corner café.

• Have an impromptu sleepover in the tent or have a family camp-out in front of the fireplace.

• Make a family love bug. Use a small pompom, add some feet, goggle eyes, and antennae. Secretly put the bug in a place to surprise someone in the family—in a briefcase, the silverware drawer, the cookie jar, someone's shoe. When the bug is found, the person knows that someone loves him/her and is thinking about him/her. Then he/she can hide the bug for another family member.

• Organize the family photo collection.

• Blow bubbles together.

• Go for a walk and take the dog.

• Teach the dog a new trick.

• Call grandparents or other special people and ask how their day was.

• Make a family band. Put beans between two tin pie plates, use an oatmeal box for a drum, play a comb. Write a family song and play it.

- Put on a family talent show.
- Have a dress-up box with old clothes and put on a play.
- Play school and let the kids be the teacher.
- Have a kid-size tea party.
- Take a picture of the family and make a frame out of popsicle sticks, shells, bottle caps, or buttons.
- Make a necklace or bracelet out of cereal and then eat it.
- Collect all of the loose change around the house, in the washer, between the couch cushions, etc., and buy a family treat.
- Hold a power outage party. Pretend that the electricity is off and play games by candlelight.
- Hold a family night Olympics, such as setting up a miniature golf course in the basement constructed of boxes, cans, old pieces of carpet and wood, etc.
- Sleep under the stars.
- Save all the underwear and socks to fold during a family movie.
- Go to the community-wide or school open-swim night.
- Build a model.
- Go fishing.
- Start a family hobby.
- Put together a jigsaw puzzle.
- Rent a family video and make popcorn.
- Watch one of your favorite old movies with your children.
- Organize a neighborhood potluck.
- Play charades: write down movie or book titles on small slips of paper, take turns drawing a name, and act it out for the other members of your team.
- Do something active: bike, hike, walk, play basketball, or play tag or Frisbee.

• Try family bowling, roller-skating, mini-golf, tennis, canoeing, or rock climbing.
• Have family races: running, three-legged, with an egg on a spoon. Have everyone eat soda crackers. The winner is the first to whistle.
• Welcome someone coming home from work by drawing beautiful pictures on the sidewalk with chalk.

Seasonal Fun

• Build a snow animal or sand sculpture.
• If you live where there is snow, build a snow slide.
• In warm weather, have a family water fight.
• Rake an elderly neighbor's leaves or shovel their walk in the winter.
• Play hopscotch with all the neighborhood kids.
• In warm weather, join the kids running through the sprinkler.

Holiday Fun

• At special holidays like Thanksgiving, Christmas, Chanukah, or Kwanza, have each extended family member share their most memorable holiday story.
• Make a holiday item for someone who can't get out, such as a valentine or May basket.
• Share New Year's Eve with the children, snuggled up in front of the fireplace, and recap favorite moments of the past year. Make new commitments for the New Year.
• Try heart-shaped meatloaf for Valentine's Day.
• Serve green food for St. Patrick's Day.
• On April Fools' Day, eat dinner backward, starting with dessert.

• Tell scary stories on Halloween and have a meal cooked in a pumpkin. Have a traditional "blowing out the candle in one breath from the furthest distance" contest.

• Choose names for Secret Santa. Each person does really nice things for their Secret Santa for the ten days before Christmas. Secretly make their bed, take their turn doing the dishes, slip a note under their pillow, etc.

Birthday Fun

• To save time and conserve resources, instead of wrapping gifts, leave them in their bags and hide them around the house. Play "you're getting hot, you're getting cold" with the birthday child until the gifts are found.

• Have the birthday child wake up to "The String Thing." Tie a bright-colored string to the birthday child's doorknob. In the morning, the child must follow the string all over the house to the place where a small gift is hidden.

• Let the birthday person choose his or her favorite dinner and where it is to be eaten. It may be in lunch boxes in the tree house!

Kitchen Fun

• Make homemade pizza as a family with frozen bread dough and toppings.

• Bake cookies together and deliver them to an elderly neighbor or shut-in.

• For dessert, have everyone finger-paint with pudding.

• Cook for the season: applesauce in the fall, a gingerbread house at Thanksgiving, etc.

- Create an ethnic dish: lefse (Norwegian bread), körv (Swedish sausage), potato pancakes (Jewish), cabbage rolls (German or Polish), and so forth.
- Hide a jelly bean in a dinner dish. Whoever finds it gets to stay up fifteen minutes longer than usual and have special time with Mom and Dad.

Home Projects

- Who can pull the most weeds?
- Rake a huge pile of leaves. Then jump in them before bagging them.
- Everyone shovels snow into a huge pile, then tunnels through it to build a fort. (For safety, make sure it isn't too close to the road.)
- Have a clean-up-the-room party (family room, laundry room, etc.).
- Have everyone help plant and tend a family garden.
- Hold a clean-out-the-garage event. Sell unused items and put the money toward a family outing.
- Have a family wash-the-dog party.

· 6 ·

Planes, Trains, and Automobiles: Reclaiming Family Outings and Vacations

When the Dohertys' youngest child, Elizabeth, was no longer interested in bedtime talks at age thirteen, Bill felt that he had lost an important way of connecting with his daughter. But about a week later, Elizabeth suggested that she and her father go out to the Dairy Queen. "Just the two of us?" Bill inquired. "Yes, just us. We can ask Mom and Eric if they want us to bring something home for them." Off they went, father and daughter, to eat ice cream and talk. The next week, Elizabeth made the same suggestion. And then the next week. Eventually, they agreed that they would aim to do a Dairy Queen trip every week, deciding each week what was possible in their schedules. Sometimes Elizabeth had an agenda for these outings, something she was worrying about or curious about. Other times they talked about nothing in particular. But they both knew that these trips were not primarily about ice cream. They did them every week for five years, until Elizabeth went off to college. In January in Minneapolis, they were sometimes the only people at the Dairy Queen on Hennepin Avenue.

When Elizabeth was fourteen, she noticed a copy of *The Family Therapy Networker* magazine on the kitchen table. The cover photo depicted sullen teenagers. Noticing her interest, Bill suggested that she read the articles and give him her reaction. After reading intently, Elizabeth was angry. She felt that the articles were entirely negative about teenagers and offered few ideas about how to make things better. Bill suggested that she write a letter to the editor, which she did. The letter was published and received a lot of attention because of its point of view and the age of the writer. In fact, one well-known family therapist used to quote from this letter when he spoke to parents of teens. Elizabeth had learned an important lesson about speaking out.

When she turned twenty, the same magazine had another cover story on teenagers. The editor called Bill to ask him if his daughter might be willing to review this issue and see if they had done a better job. (He had agreed with her critique of the previous issue.) Elizabeth was heading off to Scotland for study abroad, but agreed to read the articles on the plane and send an e-mail as soon as she arrived in Scotland, in order to meet the magazine's deadline. Here is her letter to the editor of *The Family Therapy Networker:*

> I am the 14-year-old, now 20, who wrote the letter six years ago critiquing your previous issue on teens. Thank you for your more positive look at teenagers in your May/June 1996 issue. The articles were less judgmental about kids and offered more ideas about how parents and therapists can work with them. The articles were also more compassionate towards parents who themselves face a confusing set of expectations for raising teenagers. I especially appreciated Ron Taffel's article "Second Family," which offered specific strategies for working with teenagers' own communities.

In the last six years, I have come to feel strongly that parents need to spend one-to-one time with their teenagers. Ritualized time together, however long or short, allows trust to build in a healthy, deliberate manner. The ritual time I shared with my father (every night at bedtime until age 13, then ice cream out once a week) helped me connect with him as a respectful adult and parent who, through it all, was there for me regardless of whether I felt like sharing my problems.

I am very touched that you listened so well to a letter from a critical 14-year-old, and that your latest issue on teens offered perspective and hope.

You can imagine how touched Bill was by this letter, and how reinforced he felt about his faithfulness to the ritual of going out to the Dairy Queen.

Finding the Time to Go Out and Connect

There is something about leaving the house that makes some kinds of family connections easier to make. Whether it's a walk or a leisurely drive and a trip for ice cream, leaving the distractions of the house—television, toys, phone, computer, housework—frees us up to talk and be together in different ways. Many parents of teenagers report that their teens bring up worries in the car, with both parent and child facing traffic and not each other, that do not come out at home. Some parents have found the car to be the best place to talk about sex. And many families have their greatest enjoyment on a road trip or at an amusement park, far away from the routines of the home.

The challenge is to carve out enough time for going out,

and to be intentional about connecting when you do so. Being too scheduled with individual activities makes it hard to have spontaneous outings. You can't wake up on a Saturday morning and say "Let's head to the lake" when most Saturday mornings are committed to individual activities such as dance recitals and sports events. Of course, the same is true if the parents' work schedules spill over into evenings and weekends. If going out always has an external purpose—to get somewhere for an event—it's not the same as going out for enjoyment and connection.

You may argue, as some parents do, that one-to-one time in the car on the way to children's events can indeed be a connecting form of going out. As we said above, this can be true, just as taking a child shopping for new clothes can be an opportunity for one-to-one time. Everyday life is filled with opportunities for parent-child conversation and closeness if we take advantage of them. But there is a big difference between driving to the Dairy Queen or to a movie or to pick apples, and driving at the last minute to a piano practice or hockey game. In addition to time pressure, the main difference is that, in a going-out ritual, you all know that the purpose is to have fun together, as opposed to accomplishing some task or getting to a destination. Random moments of connection while driving somewhere are to be treasured, but you can't count on them as a way to connect with a child—especially now that so many kids prefer to wear their own earphones or watch a video in the backseat of the SUV.

Going-out rituals can be with the whole family or with subgroups. Tom, now a middle-aged father, remembers with fondness the outings he and his father took to Minnesota Twins baseball games. It was just father and son, in the illuminated ballpark under the stars (this was before domed stadiums). It was his special time with his dad, a connection they did not experience in the same way at home.

Barbara and her family evolved a similar mother-daughter ritual. When their oldest daughter turned four and was presented with twin siblings, Barbara knew that she had to find special time just for this daughter. So she started a ritual of attending local children's theater productions with her daughter. But as the twins grew, and another child was added, the family could not afford to buy season tickets for everyone. So they started a ritual of taking turns, one child and Mom for each play. It became a cherished ritual of going out and connecting.

Going out to eat as a family is a ready-made opportunity for a ritual of connection, as long as you are deliberate. Bill's family has a pizza ritual. It started in 1986 when the Dohertys moved to Minnesota and discovered they liked the pizzas at Davanni's restaurant. They fell into a routine of going there every Friday, mostly for practical reasons: no one wanted to cook at the end of the workweek, everyone liked the pizza, and it was not expensive. Notice that it was a "routine" at first, and not a ritual, because it was not particularly significant to anyone. It was just pizza out. But Bill and Leah began to notice how much they looked forward to these outings because of the relaxed conversations that were occurring. Family members were processing their week or talking about things on their minds.

Then one night at Davanni's, thirteen-year-old Eric asked for a quarter to play a video game while the family waited for the pizza to be cooked. Bill and Leah gave him a quarter, and he later rejoined the table when the food arrived. He asked again the next week and played another game. But the third week, Bill and Leah looked at each other and said, "This defeats the purpose." That was the first time they knew there was a family purpose to this eating-out routine. Bill said to Eric, "We are not going to give you quarters for the video games anymore, because this is family time." Eric grumbled a bit but accepted the new policy.

Fifteen years later and the kids having moved from home, Davanni's is still a weekly Doherty family ritual. Mostly it was just the four Dohertys, but it also became a low-threat occasion for introducing new boyfriends or girlfriends to the parents. Nowadays, whoever brings up pizza calls around to confirm the day, and then everyone meets at Davanni's at the appointed time. In the Doherty parlance, "Let's do Davanni's" is a way of saying "Let's have some family time." In the same way, when Elizabeth wants private time with her father, she calls and says, "We haven't done ice cream for a while. How about tonight?" When you are a young person, it's a lot easier to ask for pizza or ice cream than to ask for bonding time with your parents!

We have pulled together at the end of this chapter a lot of ideas about going out and getting away to connect as a family. See what might fit for your family.

Can't Wait to Get Back on the Road Again

Nothing in family life creates such lasting memories as family trips and vacations. We will use "trips" and "vacations" interchangeably, although some families distinguish between a "trip" to visit relatives and a "vacation" for pure enjoyment. Family vacations as we think of them today are fairly new in history, mostly a twentieth-century invention. Vacations came about after the majority of people began to work for employers instead of being self-employed on the farm or in a small business. As the twentieth century progressed, more and more employers began to give paid vacations as a benefit. The advent of automobiles, as a supplement to trains and steamboats, gave families a lot more flexibility to go on a trip together. Even at that, it was mostly wealthy and upper-middle-class families who could afford vacations until the mid-twentieth century, a time when standards of living improved for most Americans, cars became a common feature of family life, and new highways made it feasible to take long road trips. During the second half of the twentieth century, the family vacation entered the culture as an important family ritual.

It is ironic, then, that during times when standards of living have improved the fortunes of so many American families, family vacations have started to retreat. Research has shown that the number of families taking vacations declined by about 28 percent during the last two decades of the twentieth century. Furthermore, the average number of nights spent on vacations is now about five, a decrease from previous decades.

What is going on? Part of the explanation, no doubt, is dual-earner families. It's simply harder to coordinate vacation schedules when there are two working adults. But another part of the explanation is children's extracurricular schedules. Year-round sports seasons means that active children will always be playing important games and having important tournaments during summer vacation and spring break. The Sloane family, with two full-time working parents, had arranged their family vacation months in advance to occur from August 1 to August 15 at a lake cabin. But on July 28, their fifteen-year-old son's soccer team made the state tournament. After a brief hesitation, the parents canceled the family vacation because they did not want to disappoint their son or the rest of the team. The sad thing is that this may have been the last possible family summer vacation. The next year their son would be employed during the summer and would likely resist losing money for a family trip. Surrendering this important family ritual to an unexpected and unplanned youth sports event can open the door to other reasons to retreat from family time and family rituals.

But when families make vacations a priority, they rarely regret it, even when lots of things go wrong. Like all other extended family rituals (like weddings and the holiday season rituals), family vacations generally involve periods of tension and irritability. But those very frustrations often become the fondest memories in later years. We think of the family whose North Carolina vacation was spent fleeing a hurricane, or the family who spent half of its vacation in car repair shops. These became raucously funny stories years later. Even the nonstop "when are we going to get there?" questions from children become mirthful memories when the children are grown.

Vacations imprint collective memories into the consciousness of family members. Barbara's family developed two kinds of vacation rituals—one with the whole family and one separated by gender. This tradition began when the men in the family decided to go on a real cattle drive. Barbara realized that in many families, the father and sons go on trips together for male bonding. Why not the females? So Barbara and her daughters created "girl trips." They took off in the car, stopping whenever they wanted—to shop, for a fudge break, to smell the flowers, or to visit a museum. No need for a cross-gender consensus! They would have long lunches, stay up late chatting and laughing till they cried. The men reported similarly good bonding experiences, doing completely different things.

Carol tells about the joys of car trips:

> Although our kids are older now (nineteen and twenty-two), their favorite vacations have always been the car trips—especially the long car trips we have taken. We always bought treats for the car that we otherwise didn't have much at home. We avoided fast food on trips

because, interestingly, it wasn't much of a treat! We fixed sandwiches in the car or stopped at a park or rest stop along the way to eat. The kids LOVED it!

Reading has always been a big part of our trips. We'd get maps and guidebooks from AAA and enjoy reading about each little town as we passed through. But the biggest hit for us was always listening to Books on Tape as we drove. We'd get the unabridged editions so they were sometimes fifteen to eighteen hours of listening. You can get them at the library or order them through the Books on Tape company. Sometimes we read books relating to what we would see (we were all mesmerized by *The Killer Angels* on the way to Gettysburg a few years ago), but we sometimes just got good adventures the whole family would enjoy—Jack London, Mark Twain, or John Grisham. They always evoked great family discussions. And the biggest bonus for us? We rarely heard the words, "Are we there yet?"

Notice in Carol's story that the best memories of vacations were not so much the places they went as the journey on the way. There is something about being cooped up with family for days on end that can bring out the creativity in parents and kids to make the best of the time. Bill's kids used to look for states' license plates on the road, or count windmills. Leah had a great solution to the "how long till we're there?" questions. Each child got three times to ask the question on any day's trip. The result? They saved them up and didn't even ask their three questions.

Sue Kakuk, whose stories we have told before, also likes books as part of vacations. And notice how her family uses a vacation photograph as a way to sustain the memories and share the experience with others.

I try to find a book that has subject matter about our destination and then read it out loud in the evenings. For example, while canoeing in the [Minnesota/Canada] Boundary Waters, we read *Chasing Bears* and while visiting the Grand Canyon, we read *Down River*. It started on one of our first camping trips. When you are all crammed together in a tent with little privacy, it seemed a natural thing to do. Now, even when we stay in the comfort of a nice hotel, it is a nice excuse to turn the TV off and connect again before retiring in the evening. I also try to keep a journal and then we reread it before we go on our next vacation. We always take a family photo and use one for our Christmas card or newsletter.

Sue also discovered a valuable principle about family rituals, one that is particularly important for vacations: maximum participation by all family members.

This past week, we have anxiously been preparing for a camping vacation to the Upper Peninsula of Michigan. A few years ago, I would have done all the prep work, organizing, packing, etc., all by myself. I also wouldn't sleep many nights with so many things on my mind. This year I involved my kids (ages ten and thirteen) a lot more than normal. We went grocery shopping together. They personally picked out their favorite crackers, juice, yogurt, etc. (They also bagged and helped unload!) They made the cookies. They made the GORP! My daughter is writing checklists for everyone. We all looked at the map together to figure out the best way. Should we travel the shortest mileage or take the "quickest" route? I am looking forward to the trip. We have all taken responsibility in the plan-

ning. I know things won't be perfect. I will share the good
and the not so good, when we get back.

The good and not so good—that sums up realities of family
life and family trips and vacations. They are periods of intense
family interaction, bringing out the best and worst in us. But fortunately, most of the memories are of the best.

When we think of family life, most of us think first of hearth
and home. But family life is also about what we do outside the
home and away from the neighborhood, in those hours or days
when we are freed temporarily from the constraints of home life,
when we experience nature together or learn something together
or play together. It will be a terrible loss for the next generation if
we allow our frantic schedules to interfere with this dimension of
family life. Going out and going away are prisms through which
we see our families refracted in a different light, with colors we do
not see at home.

Tips for Family Fun When Going Out or Away

Getting Out Around Home

- If grandparents are nearby, set up a regular "play date" with them.
- Visit free sites: parks, beaches, playgrounds. Take a picnic.
- Get away under your own power: walk, hike, bike, rock climb, or canoe.
- Have a regular "meal out" time. It gives the cook a break and everyone can concentrate just on each other.

• Have a dollar date. Split the family into teams and visit a mall. Set the timer and each team must find the perfect gift for the other team.

• Visit your local zoo, arboretum, science museum, or children's theater.

• Go to the library on a mission! Do research on your next vacation destination, stock up on books for your next trip, or do research on an animal that you expect to visit at the zoo.

• Turn home chores into family projects: visit the tree nursery, the paint store, the hardware store, etc.

• Have a New Year's family meeting to discuss ideas for vacations for the coming year. Don't forget about trips near home.

Getting Away

• On longer trips, take special snacks that you usually don't have at home.

• In the car, start a family choir and sing everyone's favorites as you travel.

• When children are old enough, read chapter books on road trips.

• Get the whole family involved in your next vacation. Check out books, maps, and brochures about the place you will be visiting. Have each family member do research on what he or she wants to see or do and present it to the family.

• On a long road trip, draw Secret Pal names. Try to do secret random acts of kindness for that person. For example, carry your pal's suitcase, pay for a special dessert, let him or her in the bathroom first, find a special rock or shell and hide it in his or her backpack, write a note and put it under your pal's pillow.

• On longer trips, pack a fun bag for each child. They aren't allowed to open it until the plane is in the air or the car begins to roll. Accumulate "doing" items like paper, markers, crayons, and Play-Doh. Add a few treats, small games, and toys.

• Pack a special backpack with games that can only be played with on trips.

• Keep a travel journal. Write down everyone's favorite and not so favorite moments. Read this journal before your next vacation. It brings back good memories.

• Bring along appropriate books with you to read before bedtime.

• Take tapes of favorite songs, and sing along.

• Play car games like:

Guess the number of cars on the approaching train and then count them to see who wins.

Play the Alphabet Game. Take turns going through the entire alphabet by finding a corresponding item with that letter: apple tree, barn, cow, door, etc.

Take turns playing the alphabet game by finding letters in license plates.

Keep track of license plates from different states.

Make up your own stories. One person starts with the first sentence and each person takes turns adding to it. You will end up with a pretty funny story!

• Let each child who is old enough pack his or her own suitcase. Help by making a list of what should be packed—

necessities like underwear (how many?), toothbrush, floss, appropriate attire such as three long-sleeved shirts, four short-sleeved, two pairs long pants, three pairs shorts. Anything beyond the necessities is their responsibility.

• Order kids' meals on airplanes when you order the tickets.

7

Taming the Technology Beast:
Reclaiming Family Life in the Home

Time famine in contemporary family life is not just about over-scheduling ourselves and our children. It's also about the power of electronic technologies, particularly television, video games, CD players, computers, and the Internet. These media technologies can be used to enhance family connections, but in practice they tend to isolate family members from one another by creating electronic cocoons. No plan for reclaiming family life in today's world can ignore media technology in the home. To put today's challenge in perspective, here is a summary from the Kaiser Family Foundation's landmark study on children and media, published in 1999:

> Today's kids spend more time with more media than any generation before them, and there is every reason to assume that their media use and exposure will continue to increase. The environment of today's youth . . . is filled with media of all kinds. Their bedrooms contain televisions, print material, radios and audio systems, gaming

systems, and with growing frequency, computers. They can choose content from dozens of television channels and radio stations, hundreds of print publications, thousands of videos, and virtually an unlimited number of World Wide Web sites. . . . It is no exaggeration to say that in the U.S. today the average junior high student spends more time with media than he or she devotes to any other waking activity—they give almost 7 hours per day to media.

Using Television for Family Connection

It's easy to describe how television hurts family life, so let's start with how it can be used intentionally to promote family ties. The Carlson family had some wonderful times with a television ritual. They all watched a weekly show together; their favorites included *Scarecrow and Mrs. King, Lois and Clark,* and *Mission: Impossible.* They ate pizza and talked as they watched, knowing that the purpose was to spend time together as a family enjoying something they liked on television. Bill has warm memories of his childhood family watching *The Jackie Gleason Show* on Saturday nights. It was the only show that even his father, a critic of television, liked to watch, and Bill can still picture his father's hearty Irish laughter at Jackie Gleason's antics.

As a parent, you can sometimes pick up on a special one-to-one opportunity to connect around a television show. Bill's daughter Elizabeth loved *The Wonder Years;* Kevin, the main character, was her age. Bill and Elizabeth watched the program together many Tuesday nights, talking about it during commercials and afterward.

The key to making television viewing a family ritual is to be intentional about it, deciding what to watch, and doing it together. Cuddling up helps. The same goes for videos. Young children love to watch their favorite videos over and over with their parents. Although Peter's children were too young to see the scary movie *Jurassic Park* in the theater, they bought the video and found the dinosaurs less scary on the small screen with a parent in the same room. It became a favorite family ritual, with the kids anticipating every line of dialogue and every move of the dinosaurs.

Leslie and her family also used videos to enhance a special family vacation. Here is her story:

> When we took a trip with some exchange students from Spain, we took some videos with us that we could play on the VCR as we traveled. They were set in the areas that we were visiting: *Dances With Wolves* for South Dakota, *North by Northwest* for Mount Rushmore, *Close Encounters of the Third Kind* for Devils Tower, and *Jeremiah Johnson* in Wyoming. We had some great discussions about culture and history at dinner each evening.

Breaking the TV Trance

The main problem with television for family life is that it is simply on too much. The majority of families keep it on whenever they are home, including during rituals like dinner. If the television turned itself off automatically after each show, requiring us to turn it back on to watch another show, television would probably be less intrusive. Most people don't say, "Let's turn the television on during meals." It's just that they don't turn it off. The TV is the great absorber of family attention, the great distracter from conversations.

We all know this, but many of us don't notice the trancelike state that television induces in children and adults alike. Have you ever tried to get your children's (or spouse's) attention while they are watching television? They are in a trance, a state of consciousness more like daydreaming than being awake. When spoken to, the person in the TV trance invariably either fails to respond or says, "What?"

Unrestrained television watching not only degrades family connections, it also hurts community connections. Robert Putnam, in his book *Bowling Alone,* documents how the onset of television helped to bring about a decline in people's engagement with their neighbors and community. We have our own entertainment centers in our homes (even more so now with fancy audio equipment to accompany television), and we don't feel we need our neighbors for enjoyment. Putnam describes how communities in the Arctic Circle experienced a drastic decline in civic engagement after they got television. One community had a decades-long ritual where families gathered in the town civic center every Thursday for conversation and activities. Within weeks of the arrival of the TV signal via satellite, the town hall gathering had evaporated.

You no doubt have heard all of the advice about limiting television in the home: decide in advance what you will watch and allow your children to watch, set time limits, be aware of what your kids watch, turn it off during dinner, don't use television as a babysitter or as a reward for good behavior. The trick is pulling these things off in a culture where television watching seems like an inalienable right. Here are some strategies parents we know have tried.

Jane describes how her family experimented with unplugging the television:

> A family activity that we would strongly encourage is more of a nonactivity. We decided about two years ago to do an experiment to help us find more time to spend together. Our children were about five and one at the time. We simply

unplugged the TV and announced that it was broken and that we would have to find other things to do for the month. We rediscovered card and board games, reading books and magazines, walks, parks, and even going to bed earlier to get that all-important sleep so many adults and children need. We have since plugged the TV back in but it is rarely on anymore and even then for PTV [public television] or a video.

Bugs Peterschmidt decided to get serious about all media, beginning with television.

We're trying an experiment this summer—I call it "unplugged" summer although that's not totally true. I think our kids (thirteen and ten) are pretty typical in that they cannot regulate themselves when it comes to turning off a screen—any screen! When I would say, "Ten more minutes, then you need to shut it off," the ten minutes would turn into a battle of wits and wills. I decided those battles were taking up precious minutes we weren't ever getting back again, so now we have a "no media rule" until after dinner. They get an hour a day—they decide how to spend the hour. If they want to check e-mail, watch a show, or play a video game, they have to choose how to spend that hour. I am trying to be unplugged until after supper, and I think it is as difficult for me as well. One of the hidden benefits I found is that I don't subject myself to commercials that show perfect-looking women being perfectly satisfied with some perfect product or experience that I shouldn't live without. I'm feeling a little calmer. I like the quiet.

Notice the strategy here of setting hour limits but giving the kids freedom of choice within that time frame. This keeps the parent from telling children to stop watching a show ten minutes before it ends, leading to endless arguments. Also, the rule about no media until after dinner simplifies monitoring.

Sometimes there are negative side effects of efforts to limit television. Here is Griff Wigley's account of what his family tried:

> When we cut our kids down to two hours per week, they spent another three hours a week poring over the TV guides to decide how they were going to spend their two hours. Aarrrgghhh! That was the last straw.

Griff and his wife tried many other schemes with their four children, many of them successful for a time. And then they bit the big bullet:

> We finally just decided to turn it off completely for us and them. This was eleven years ago . . . they were fourteen, twelve, nine, and five at the time. We still rented videos and didn't try to restrict their TV watching at their friends' houses. It made a huge difference in all our lives—I was one of the biggest offenders—and we still don't watch it. The one problem, in retrospect, is that it made it harder for them to convince friends to hang out at our house. I'm really not sure if I'd do it again the same way.

Griff's story shows how there are no easy answers in a society that is so preoccupied with television. Ban it and your kids and their friends spend time elsewhere. Limit it and you could spend your time policing the policy. But it seems that parents do best when they set up straightforward limits that are easily enforceable. Sue took a chance on pairing TV time with reading time, and fortunately the outcome was that her son became more mindful of his television use, and he read more. She begins by honestly admitting that she had fallen into using the television as a babysitter so that she could get housework done, a temptation nearly every parent has given in to from time to time.

> I started taking advantage of my son escaping to the basement family room and not bothering me for quite some time. Boy, could I get things done! He admitted he watched too much TV and was willing to make a change. Here is what we came up with: He gets half an hour of TV a day, free. To earn more TV hours he has to read. For every half hour of reading, he earns half an hour of TV. I was a little worried that I might have to put a limit on the amount of TV, but it is working out to about one and a half hours of reading for the same amount of TV. That isn't bad. Yes, he is doing more reading (my goal), but also he is being responsible about keeping track of TV hours. He isn't challenging me on the deal.

Perhaps Sue and her son have captured the key ingredient in preventing television from dominating family life: making conscious choices and keeping track of those choices. Different families will end up with different degrees of television use, but if they are intentional about it, they are likely to find a balance that works to the advantage of their family time and family connections.

Competing with Computers and the Internet

Of the new technologies, the computer hooked to the Internet is changing family life most quickly. As everyone knows, this technology opens up the world to a child. Knowledge about nearly everything is literally at your child's fingertips; it makes us think of the biblical tree of the knowledge of good and evil. Type "Whitehouse.gov" on the keyboard and learn about the workings of the executive branch of the federal government. Type the wrong suffix after "White House" and you get a Dutch pornography site. Access one Web site for an encyclopedia that helps you research a term paper, and another Web site to download a plagiarized term paper.

Chat rooms and instant messaging have become preoccupations with younger and younger children. At their best, these forms of communication give kids a fun way to connect with their friends and with other kids from different places and environments. Learning Spanish? You can easily have a daily pen pal from Spain or Latin America. Want to hang out with friends on a cold winter evening without leaving home? Talk to them all at once in a chat room.

Most parents are becoming aware of the risks of these communication technologies to their children. Child predators in chat rooms top the list, but too much time and preoccupation with e-mailing, instant messaging, and Web surfing are also bad for kids. We are focusing here on something not in the forefront of many parents' minds: how being absorbed in communicating with others outside the home on the computer can create more distance in the home. Some kids run from school to several after-school activities (with a drive-by dinner thrown in) to the computer for e-mail and instant messaging, then to homework and back to the computer before bed to get updates from friends. Little time is left for conversations with parents or siblings.

It's not just the kids, of course. The invasion of the adult work world in the form of evening and weekend e-mailing by parents adds to the problem. We have the technology to communicate easily with everyone but our families. Family communication is a low-tech activity in a high-tech world.

But it doesn't have to be this way. We buy computers and information technology, and we can control them. The first and most important step is to not allow computers in children's rooms. Keep them in public places in the house so that you can use the computer there yourself (thereby limiting the child's access) and look informally at the screen as you pass by. The same is true for televisions in children's bedrooms. Did you know that 25 percent of preschoolers have a television in their bedroom? By age seven, 40 percent do, and the percentages keep going up into adolescence.

When we allow our children to have access to information technology in their bedrooms, we put them at much higher risk for accessing harmful material and for being preyed upon by adults who would hurt them. But beyond these obvious risks to children, we also isolate them from the rest of the family. As children reach the teen years, when a degree of withdrawal from parents is developmentally normal, we give them little incentive to be around the rest of the family when their bedrooms are fully stocked entertainment and communication centers.

You might ask, Why try to force teens to be with the family when they want their solitude? We confess that this attitude among some parents really puzzles us. Why not give teens a stocked refrigerator and hot plate to prepare their meals, and an outside entrance to their room? There is a big difference between dragging kids out of their rooms and forcing family conversation, and creating opportunities and incentives for hanging out with the family. Placing the television in a family room creates such opportunities and incentives, as does the computer in a hallway off the kitchen. Teens will find ways to get their privacy needs met without parents handing them a message that says, "We're here only if you spontaneously feel like communicating with us. Otherwise, entertain yourself on electronic equipment we have purchased for you."

Technology Giveth and Technology Taketh Away

Just when we start to despair over families losing the battle over family time to technology, along comes a new technology that families can use mindfully to tame the television. We are referring to digital television replay boxes that promise to transform the way Americans watch television. These devices allow for up to 320 hours of recording television shows, which can be played back whenever the viewer wants to watch them. The boxes keep track of television preferences and automatically record shows without being programmed. Recording and playback are far easier than for VCR, which many people have never mastered beyond putting in a video and watching it. Michael Lewis, author of the book *Next: The Future Just Happened,* maintains that these digital replay boxes will put viewers in charge of when they watch television, because they will no longer be tethered to the time a show airs.

Once again, it's a good news/bad news scenario with this groundbreaking technology, which media experts believe will replace VCRs in American homes. The bad news is that early surveys indicate that people who have these devices spend more hours watching television, probably because they never miss their favorite shows. The good news comes in the form of a new opportunity to control what a family watches. It seems that the early purchasers of the replay boxes rarely watch television shows as they come in live on their television sets. They store them on the boxes and watch them when it's convenient. What this means is that parents will have the technology to allow children to watch only prerecorded programs that they have given permission for. In other words, the television can be permanently turned off as a live source of programs. Parents can reclaim the family media schedule. If children try to program extra hours, it is easy for parents to check to see which shows the box is planning to tape. As a bonus, commercials can be skipped with this technology, a blessing to many parents and something probably missed by the children. Needless to say, the digital replay boxes can be used by parents themselves to gain control over their own tendency to zone out and watch one show after another of scheduled television.

Our point is that as parents we can be alert to how technology can help us master technology, and we can use it to promote family connections. Look at how e-mail has helped college students and their parents stay in touch, and even share feelings and observations that might be too threatening face-to-face. Griff gives his young adult sons glimpses into his personal life via occasional e-mail excerpts from his journal. They can choose whether or not to read them or initiate a discussion about them. He also regularly opens an instant message window on his PC so that when they're at their computers, they can spontaneously check in with one another throughout the week, even though they are hundreds of miles apart. He finds that using these technologies is deepening his relationship with them in unexpected ways.

The more we wire our houses, the less we connect with one another in our families. But that is not the fault of the technologies. It's our fault for not being proactive about taming these beasts. Imagine our houses and neighborhoods taken over by wild dogs who had entered the human environment but never became domesticated. Their presence and actions would diminish the quality of our world. But we know that humans and dogs have lived together in relative peace and mutual affection for millennia; for many of us, dogs are like members of our families. It's because we humans grew to understand them and learned to live with them, and taught them how to live with us. We can do the same with technology, the newest "pet" in the human family, which could threaten our deepest bonds if we let it, but can nurture our deepest bonds if we make sure that family life is first.

8

Putting Family First
in Two-Parent Families

In the Maloney family, Emily was the parent who advocated for family dinner rituals. Dinners were important in her growing-up years, and she wanted the same for her family now. Her husband, Bruce, was not against family dinners, but they were not a priority for him. As their three boys grew up and pushed the limits of the dinner ritual—by coming late or scheduling activities during this hour—Emily protested while Bruce made excuses for them. (Children, of course, know instinctively when their parents are not together on an expectation, and take advantage.) The boys complained of being hungry and tended to "graze" before Dad got home, rather than waiting to have dinner as a family. They lobbied to keep the television on while eating. Even if Mom had turned it off, Dad sometimes clicked the television back on when he got home, if there was something he wanted to catch in the news. Over time, Bruce joined the children in passive resistance to what he saw as his wife's rigidity about family dinners.

Eventually, Emily gave up and became a TV-watching grazer herself. But she felt sad and guilty about it, and irritated with her husband. Then Emily attended a public lecture on the importance of family dinners. Now angry at herself for giving up, she declared one evening to the rest of her family that things had to change. "We will revive family meals," she announced, "starting with Sunday dinners. We will make Sunday dinners special." Her husband was quiet during her speech; the boys were sullen.

When the next Sunday night came around, the pro football game was in sudden death overtime at the appointed dinner hour. Bruce and the boys pleaded for a delay. The chicken began to dry out in the oven. Neither team scored on their first possession. The rice began to congeal, as Emily's own pot began to boil. Finally, everyone sat down to a surly meal. Do you think Emily will keep to her resolution about Sunday dinners in the future? Forget about it.

Two-parent families are often the best, but are sometimes the worst, environment for children to grow up in. If you live in a two-parent family, you have the advantage of another committed adult to support you in raising your children. You have someone at hand to talk things over with, to share decision making, and to help shoulder the workload. Your children have a model of adults working together for the good of others.

You also know what can go wrong when parents don't raise children as a team. If parents pull in different directions, then the rules of mathematics are violated: one plus one equals less than one parent. Two parents undermining each other have a harder time raising responsible children than one competent parent.

When it comes to making family life the top priority, the main question is whether you and your spouse share similar values about how to make use of family time. Take the Schneider family. Marvin is trying to put more balance into the family's schedule. He had not minded being so busy, but now that the kids are being invited to join traveling sports teams, he is in favor of cutting back. Sarah, his wife, sees herself as much more in touch with what contemporary children need. She knows what activities the neighbors have their children involved in, and she wants nothing less for her own daughters. When Sarah and Marvin argue about the upcoming decision to enroll their twelve-year-old daughter, Rachel, in a traveling soccer team, Sarah implies that Marvin is too lazy to put himself out for his child. And not every child, she explains, is good enough to be invited to try out for this team. Her best friends are trying out. At least let her find out if she is good enough to make the team.

Marvin, for his part, believes intuitively that family time should have a higher priority in their lives, but he can't articulate this value very well. Rather, he focuses on the inconvenience of the traveling schedule, the pressure it books on the weekends, and a general worry that their daughter will be too busy. Sarah, like most mothers, is the designated family leader on parenting matters. She does not take Marvin's objections seriously, answering each like a good debater. The traveling season is a great opportunity to get out of town and socialize with other families. Their daughter is never happier than when she is busy; she doesn't have enough time to worry about things. Sarah wins hands down, and Marvin grumpily goes along.

If Marvin had been better able to articulate the values we are upholding in this book, the marital disagreement would have been on more even footing. It would have contrasted two legitimate goals: the goal of Rachel having meaningful outside activities and the goal of having a balanced family life with enough time for family activities and the opportunity to hang out. In two-parent families, when one parent loses sight of the family's needs for time and joint activities, it's up to the other parent to raise the family flag and keep it there. But you've got to raise a flag of values and ideals, not just one of convenience or vague worries. Most parents will set aside inconvenience for the sake of their children's opportunities, and vague concerns about being overbusy don't compete with the tangible rewards of outside activities. You've got to keep your eye on the prize of a balanced, connected family life and enough time for children to be children. Those are values worth struggling for in a two-parent family.

Shared leadership worked better in another family where the father, previously a champion swimmer, was pushing his son into increasingly competitive swim programs. Daniel, the eight-year-old son, was showing stress symptoms in school—headaches, stomachaches—but would never tell his dad he wanted to back off on the swimming. Dad bragged to anyone who would listen about how his son was more advanced than Dad was himself at age eight. He dismissed his wife's concerns about how tired and preoccupied the boy was getting, and how he did not seem to be enjoying swimming, excellent though he was. Finally, the mother leveraged the concerns of the school counselor to confront her husband about his obsession with their son's swimming. The father agreed to a low-key conversation with their son in which the mother gently asked him if he would like to cut back next season on swimming. Looking warily at his father, the boy quietly said, "Yes, that would be okay." To his credit, this father did a turnaround in his expectations of his son. But if the father had been a single parent, without a spouse to create balance, things might have gotten much worse for the boy before the father came around.

In this last scenario, the mother put her foot down and said, "Enough." It's important to be able to do this on occasion in a two-parent family. But unilateral vetoes cannot be the permanent stuff of parental teamwork. If you want to raise your children in a balanced family, you have to spend time and energy getting on the same page with your spouse. Otherwise, you will win some battles but eventually lose the war to today's frenetic, competitive culture, which may be too strong for one parent alone to resist if the other parent is in its embrace. If your spouse will not work with you on these important concerns, then get some help from a family therapist. The stakes are too high for your children.

How to Be a Parental Team
That Puts Family First

Here are some ideas about working together with your co-parent, gleaned from our personal and professional experience.

• *Talk openly together* about the values you hold concerning family life, and what you think about the balance between family time and outside activities. Don't assume you see things the same way or hold the same values in the same priority order.

• *Clarify your parenting values* by discussing specific aspects of family time—meals, bedtimes, attendance at religious activities, vacations.

• *Talk specifically about the themes we have been discussing in this book.* Do you both see a tendency in your community toward scheduled hyperactivity? Toward excessive competition in childhood? Are these a threat to your own family?

• *Look for your differences and put them on the table.* Does one of you tend to be looser about family time and family rituals, while the other is stricter? Is one more gung ho about outside activities for the children? Try to surface these differences without making one parent the bad parent. Talk about where in your backgrounds your differences might come from. There may be value in both perspectives.

• *Agree that you will be a united front with the children.* Be committed to work with, and sometimes blend, your parenting differences.

• *Both of you should support and enforce the final decisions.* Once you have agreed on expectations of your children, you should be interchangeable in carrying them out. If bedtime is at 8:30, both parents should enforce it, even if one feels more strongly about it.

• *Experiment with switching roles.* If you find yourselves getting locked into "enforcer" versus "easygoing" roles with the children when it comes to family time and rituals, deliberately plan a period of time to reverse these roles. For example, let the easygoing parent take over getting the children ready for bed or saying no to excessive overnights with friends.

• *Disagree in private.* If you have concerns about your partner's parenting behavior or decisions, talk about them in private rather than undermining the partner in front of the children.

• *Carve out time for your own relationship.* We devote chapter 11 to this important point.

Children cling not only to their parents, but to their parents' relationship with each other. Loving, cooperative two-parent families are clearly the best environment for today's children to be raised in. But having two parents in the home does not ensure that they will work together to raise good citizens. Even parents with similar values have to be good negotiators.

The Art of Negotiating Changes with Your Co-parent

Most of us get used to things the way they have been in our families, even if the way they have been is not always satisfying. Family routines and rituals take on a life of their own. If your family celebrates Christmas, try to change the time your family opens Christmas presents and you are asking for a battle. Change can also be difficult if the family's patterns give individual family members maximum freedom, as in family meals on the fly rather than being organized, or visits to relatives that are optional for the children, or children going to bed whenever they please. For these two reasons—the weight of tradition and the desire to preserve independence—family rituals are difficult to create or modify. And the biggest challenge may be your co-parent, who, as an adult, may not be interested in changing to suit newfangled ideas you got from some book!

The most immediate risk you face when recommending cutting back on outside activities or creating new rituals is that your co-parent might see you as being controlling. The result is that your whole family may react negatively before they even consider your idea on its merits. In the area of marital time, for example, if you suggest to your spouse that it might be nice if you both start going to bed at the same time, you are likely to get an elaborate defense of your partner's different sleep needs and a criticism of your own bedtime patterns. "Sure, I could go to bed at eight o'clock with you every night, and then lie there and stare at the ceiling fan till midnight while you snore." If you announce to your dinner-grazing teenagers that you want more family dinners, and you have not worked out an agreement with your spouse in advance, you will likely hear a chorus of indignant remarks about their tight schedules and the poor menu of food you prepare— and you will not have a supportive co-parent to back you up.

So what's a better way? Try starting with yourself. Clarify the needs you want to meet by a new or modified ritual and the values you want to promote. Needs and values are the best justifications for proposing that the family ship shift its course. These can be your personal needs and values, or your sense of the family's needs and values. Say that you miss the sense of family closeness you felt when the family took drives on Sunday afternoons, or played Scrabble on Saturday mornings. You wish the family could find a way to hang out and play together more.

Start with your needs and values, then, not with a direct proposal or a criticism of the status quo. If you call for change without a discussion of why a change might be helpful, you are in danger of getting into an argument about the specifics of your proposal, as when you say, "I think we should be having family dinners more often," which may be met with your spouse's response, "I can't be home for dinner every night!" Better to start by saying that you are missing family dinners because they are your favorite family time. Leave the specific solution aside for the moment. If your spouse responds defensively right away, you can deflect it by saying, "I don't know exactly what we can do. I'm just saying that I miss family dinners. How about you? Do you miss them?"

In the same way, if you start with a criticism of an outside activity that you think interferes with family time, then you are apt to elicit a defense. "We spend entirely too much time at dance recitals" will likely be met with "But Erin loves her dancing!" Start on the attack and you will get retaliation.

Here are some guidelines for constructive negotiation about family time and family rituals, drawn from Bill's book *The Intentional Family: Simple Rituals to Strengthen Family Ties*. The guidelines here are for discussions with a co-parent, but they apply to other family members as well.

1. *Choose a peaceful moment for the discussion.* It is generally a mistake to propose changes in family time use and family rituals at a moment of tension or conflict. You are apt to come across as angry and demanding. Your spouse/co-parent is likely to either give in with little intention to follow through, or resist without being open to your proposal. Instead, wait for a calm time when you both can be constructive.

2. *Say that you would like to discuss a specific outside activity or family ritual.* Tell the other that you have been thinking about this

matter, and that you want to hear his or her thoughts as well. It is generally best to tackle one activity or ritual at a time, although you can frame it in light of your overall values about family life.

3. *Say what you are feeling or needing related to the outside activity or ritual.* Examples: "I've been missing what our family dinners used to give us—a feeling of family togetherness"; "As I look at next year's schedule, I am finding myself dreading traveling soccer again because I miss having down time as a family on weekends."

4. *Invite the other person to share his or her own feelings, needs, and thoughts about the ritual.* They may be feeling the same way as you do, or quite differently. You will pick up how much openness they may feel toward changing the ritual, starting a new one, or curtailing an activity.

5. *Offer your ideas for change tentatively rather than definitively.* Once you are ready to make your proposal, keep in mind that spouses and other family members resist feeling pushed into making changes. Invite discussion rather than give commands: "Maybe we could figure out a way to have family dinners more often—not every night, but more often than we do"; "Would you be willing to talk with me about how we can spend more time together as a family on weekends?"

6. *Propose that the family gather data on what is actually going on.* One couple decided to keep a log of how many times per week they all were together for dinner. It was shocking to the reluctant parent, who then agreed to make changes.

7. *Negotiate a trial run of a solution that balances everyone's needs.* Your twelve-year-old might still play soccer, but just for six months instead of twelve, or on the local, nontraveling team. Your ten-year-old gets to choose one musical instrument from the two that she is playing now. You agree to institute a special Wednesday family night for a nice meal followed by family games, while accepting that, for now, the other weekday nights will be more chaotic.

8. *Agree to follow up to see how everyone likes a new or modified family activity.* People are more willing to try something if they feel they can escape when the new ritual does not work. And even good plans for rituals frequently require adjustments after they are lived with for a time.

These recommendations are the *direct route* to creating or changing family time patterns: bringing up your needs, values, and concerns; listening; proposing changes; gathering data; negotiating before trying something out; and evaluating how it works. A second option is the *indirect route.* "Indirect" here does not mean manipulative; it means creating an experience before proposing that it become a ritual. The indirect method of initiating or changing rituals has three steps:

1. *Make something happen one time without major comment.* You might say, "Why don't we try something different this time?" If your spouse and children go along with it, they may have a new experience they want to continue. Recall Sue from the chapter on family meals. One New Year's she moved the dinner into the dining room with the nice dishes. It was a big hit, and it introduced a new weekly ritual that involved a more elaborate meal followed by games.

2. *Ask your family how they liked the new activity and if they would like to make it part of the family's ritual in the future.* There might not have been such ready agreement if Sue had asked her husband and kids what they thought about eating a special meal in the dining room each week. Think of the indirect route to change as something akin to introducing new foods: it's often best to try something before discussing whether to add it to the family's regular menu, and sometimes it's best for the cook to prepare a new dish without announcing it in advance. The proof is in the eating—and in the ritual experience.

3. *Negotiate the specifics of the new ritual.* Ideally everyone should have input into the details of how the new or modified ritual will be incorporated into the family. In the case of Sue's family, the father offered to work with the children to prepare a special Thursday night meal, and then games got added to the mix.

A third way to initiate or change activities is the discovery method: you realize that you enjoy something you are already doing, and propose making it a ritual. As we described in chapter 6, after the Doherty family moved to Minnesota they started going to Davanni's restaurant for pizza with no thought of starting a family ritual. After several months of going every Friday night, they began to realize that they had the makings of a ritual, and decided together to commit to it as a going-out ritual of connection. A temporary routine became a family ritual. The first discussion about making it a ritual was between Bill and Leah, to make sure they were on board together.

As we have said, a loving, cooperative two-parent family is certainly the optimal environment for children and parents. But single-parent families sometimes have the advantage of clear leadership: one parent setting priorities. In two-parent families, there will always be some differences in how the parents weigh priorities about family time. They can either use these differences to create a more creative family environment for themselves and their children, or they can pull in different directions. Pulling together in making putting family first makes for a rich childhood for our kids and a satisfying parenthood for us.

9

Putting Family First
in Single-Parent Families

Single parents are subject to both blaming and patronizing in our society. The blaming takes the form of holding single mothers responsible for most social ills. The patronizing comes in language such as "heroic single parents" who do a "wonderful job" of raising children. It is true that single parenting is one of the most difficult tasks in contemporary society. But single parenting also offers the opportunity to start family life all over again, to be creative about family rituals, and to involve the children in deliberately shaping the family's values and its future. Some of the most highly intentional families we have known are single-parent families, along with some of the most overwhelmed and out-of-control. Two factors appear to distinguish the two groups: effective limit setting and the management of family time and family rituals.

Single-parent families are almost all born in the breakup of a marriage or a love affair or the unexpected loss of a spouse through death. The Jarvis family broke apart after years of Maria's struggles to get her husband, Jack, to be more involved with her and the children, nine-year-old Rick and seven-year-old Lu Anne. A skilled hands-on engineer in his work world, Jack was emotionally blank in his personal life. When Maria asked him to leave, he was devastated; he hadn't believed she was serious about her complaints. After a couple of months, Jack began to have the children over to his apartment every other weekend but he never prepared a dinner meal for them, claiming that he was completely incapable of cooking. His other child care skills were also minimal; he had left child rearing mostly to his homemaker wife during their marriage. When the children returned home to their mother's house after a visit with their father, they were wild from the lack of structure over the weekend.

Maria, for her part, was beside herself with worry about her future. With a high-school education and no relevant work skills, she didn't know how to get started with her new life. What's more, her own family had disowned her for breaking up her marriage to such a "nice man." Most of her friends were coupled friends who were now taking sides in the divorce. Sadly, as in many divorces, Maria experienced major losses in her social convoy.

Faced with these problems, Maria was just going through the motions of taking care of her children. The first casualty of the breakup was family dinners. In the past, Maria had prepared nice meals, made sure everyone was present for dinner around 6:00 P.M., and orchestrated the conversation so that the children got the chance to talk about their day. After Jack moved out, dinners were at no fixed time, Maria became a short-order cook for what each child would eat that day, and she all but stopped eating dinner herself. The times they did sit down as a threesome, the television was on and Maria did not focus the conversation as she had in the past. Maria did not make a conscious decision to stop the family dinner ritual, but a river was pulling this family south, and quickly.

The second casualty was bedtime rituals. Jack had never participated in them, and didn't know what to do when he had the kids, other than to send them off to bed or let them fall asleep in front of the television. Maria used to talk with each child at bedtime, but now she just wanted to be rid of them at the end of the day, especially because they were showing their distress by whining constantly and fighting. Because she felt guilty about neglecting a long-standing bedtime ritual, she sometimes gave in to the children's demands to be read to. But the reading was an empty ritual because of the struggle over whether to do it, and because the children, now having her attention, tried to push for more time than an exhausted Maria felt she could give. The bedtime ritual was shot and the children sought negative attention during the day as a replacement for positive attention at night.

In the midst of this awful adjustment period came an important annual family ritual: nine-year-old Rick's birthday. Still befuddled about living alone and taking care of children every other weekend, Jack expected Maria to handle the gifts and birthday party, which he expected to come home for. Maria did her traditional job of buying the presents, but did not know how to arrange the party, which traditionally had involved extended families on both sides. She was at odds with her own family and had not spoken to Jack's family since the breakup. As for having Jack over, Maria knew that Rick badly wanted his dad to be present at the party, and that Jack was not likely to have a separate party for Rick. So she invited Jack. The result was the birthday party from hell. After the cake, candles, and presents, the children clung to their dad and asked him to stay the night. Jack broke down crying and pleaded with Maria to take him back. When she refused and asked him to leave right away, she felt like the Wicked Witch of Western Connecticut. Happy birthday, Rick.

Time: The Friend and Foe of Single-Parent Families

If most American families these days suffer from a lack of family time, single-parent families suffer from time famine. Most single parents hold a job, run a household, raise children, and sometimes take classes to improve their lot. (We know moms who work two or three jobs so they can pay for extras they want their children to have, just like all the other kids.) Add to this stew our current cultural fixation on every child being busy and scheduled, and you have a prescription for meltdown. A group of single mothers that we interviewed for this book all agreed that finding time was their number one challenge. They work all day, get home, do chores, make dinner, help with homework, and then are worn out.

We know single mothers, like Diane, who are determined that their children will not miss out on opportunities afforded to children from two-parent families. What she does not realize is that many kids in two-parent families are living out-of-balance, frenetic lives. So Diane schedules her twin sons in the whole litany of activities: music lessons, soccer, gymnastics, karate, plus the children's choir at church. Diane is the only chauffeur. Evenings and weekends are a whirl of activities. Missing are quiet activities at home, family meals, bedtime rituals, and outings as a family. Because her twins' schedules are so tight, there are few visits with grandparents and other extended family, where Diane might receive some support.

For many single parents, it's damned if you do and damned if you don't. Unlike Diane, Tracie does not overschedule her nine-year-old daughter and six-year-old son. The children each have a limit of two outside activities—a music lesson and a low-key sport. The family has dinner together probably four evenings a week, and weekends are spent doing chores, running errands, and in play. How does Tracie feel about this situation? She apologizes! She wishes she could provide more opportunities for her children, she tells friends in two-parent families, but her energy level is pretty low, and she just cannot handle too crowded a schedule. She worries that her children are missing out, when in reality they have the most balanced lives in their social network.

Dawn dealt with the devastation of a husband suddenly leaving in several unique ways:

> From the beginning, I was determined to not lose "family time" following my separation and divorce. Because I treasure and recognize the necessity of family time in keeping families strong, and as the sole parent in charge, I deliberately committed myself to establishing and maintaining limits for retaining this precious commodity. One strategy that helped immensely was to get rid of the television for a couple of months as we dealt with the grief and changes that accompany divorce. Not having this numbing outlet forced my children and me to talk, cry, and play together, which fostered our healing as a family.

When asked how she dealt with outside activities as a single mom, Dawn replied:

> Simply, our finances and circumstances did not allow for many outside activities, so my sons were limited in their participation in costly sports programs and extracurricular events. We took advantage of many in-school and after-school enrichment programs as they were usually subsidized, time limited, and fostered the growth of self-esteem. . . . My determined children found ways to pursue their passions and they value these experiences highly because they contributed to making their dreams happen.

Dawn's story speaks to an ironic advantage that single parents have: *they cannot compete with two parents in today's rat race of childhood, so they are free not to try.* Far from feeling sorry for single-parent families who keep a modest outside schedule, the rest of us should learn from them.

Recasting Family Rituals After a Divorce

Not all families become disabled after a marital breakup, but most families experience significant disruption of their rituals of connection, celebration, and community. It's as if the old family script has been thrown away, and two new ones must be written. The creation of separate family rituals is a key step toward having two families that can each sustain and nurture children and be happy places for the adults.

The first challenge for single-parent families is to see themselves as real families, not just as pieces of a family. When there has been a loss, either through divorce or death, the remaining family members in the household sometimes have trouble seeing themselves as a complete family, albeit a grieving and hurting one for a time. Through therapy, Maria Jarvis came to realize that, although she felt she couldn't be married to Jack anymore, she and the children were a whole family. In addition to the stress and disorganization she was experiencing, she realized that it had not felt right to have family meals in the same way without Jack, or to go to the same pizza restaurant they had gone to as a family. That's why she felt she could not say no to Jack's coming home for the birthday party; how could birthdays be celebrated without the original family?

The challenge of feeling like a family is even greater for the "nonresidential" parent, usually the father. How do you create a sense of family every other weekend and a couple of weeks in the summer? Jack Jarvis didn't bring good parenting and family-making skills with him to his nonresidential parenting, but even if he had, the task would be daunting.

Whether you are a residential or nonresidential single parent, then, making family life the priority requires seeing yourself as a real family and acting like one in the time you have together. For the residential parent who has the children most of the time, this comes down to three strategies:

- Maintain continuity with the rituals that were working well before.
- Modify the rituals that no longer work in their original form.
- Create new rituals for the new family.

After recovering her equilibrium, Maria Jarvis did resurrect several important rituals of connection with her children. She had breakfast with her children before school and asked them about their upcoming day, she made dinner and turned the television off, and she gave each child undivided time before sleep. Children crave their traditional family rituals during times of stress and turmoil, and adults usually find them comforting as well, despite the extra work. The meals might have to be simpler, the bedtime stories not quite as long, the Sunday trips to the zoo less frequent, but continuity with past rituals of connection is crucial after a marital separation.

Maria had to modify some family rituals because Jack had filled a role she could not play or did not want to play. Almost every week, in good weather, the family used to go out for a Sunday picnic, after which Jack would play ball and wrestle with the children. Maria had no desire to become athletic at this time in her life, and this had never been her style of relating to the children. She and the children decided they would have their picnic at a different park that had swings and climbing equipment that the children could do on their own, under their mother's appreciative eye. Thus they continued an important outing ritual but in modified form.

After Maria went back to work, she felt she had too little time to talk with her children. When she got off work, she was continually chauffeuring the children from one activity to another. In this regard, she was a typical single mother. Researchers have found that single mothers have the most car trips daily of any group in the population, often under great stress and with many distractions. Maria decided to be more intentional about this driving time with her children. She created a ritual, when she was driving one child at a time, of "you tell me one thing about your day and I'll tell you one thing about mine." They would repeat the telling for as many rounds as they liked. Maria would then return to something her child might have said that needed follow-up attention.

The other ritual the family created was going out for fast food once or twice a week. What made this a ritual, and not just a fast-food eating routine, was that Maria and the children decided together which night they would go out, they alternated between two restaurants rather than arguing about where to go each time, and Maria tried to create a family discussion at the table. For the children, it was a treat they didn't get in their old family, and for Maria it was a night away from the kitchen and a time when she could focus on having a relaxed time with her children after a busy day in her new job.

Dawn also created a new ritual for her sons:

> Because we had been a family that ate meals together, we continued this practice following the divorce; only we moved meals into our dining room, as our kitchen table had moved on with my ex-husband. To deal with this sym-

bolic and painful loss, my children and I went shopping together for a new tablecloth, place mats, and napkins. Within this new setting we continued our old family ritual of holding hands and offering spontaneous prayers of thanks before meals, then talking about the day's events. . . . I continued to enlist the cooperation of my sons in food preparation and cleanup, which we did while listening to our favorite upbeat music, which always seemed to lift our spirits.

The same kind of ritual work is needed when a parent dies. In one family, when the mother died and left behind her husband and four young children, the family's ritual life collapsed almost entirely. The father at first was overwhelmed with grief and later with having to raise four children, a role he had mainly left to his wife. He clothed and fed the children, but there were practically no family rituals except for an annual trip to the cabin along with extended family. Sadly, not even the children's birthdays were routinely celebrated each year. The family's ritual life collapsed, a fact that many years later brings sadness and anger to the grown-up children. Looking back, they also realize that there had been a breakdown of support from their extended family and community, who could have intervened to help their father manage the basics of rituals such as birthdays.

In contrast to this family, Bill's friends the Skippers became even better at family rituals after the death of Cindy, Peter's wife and the mother of Cassie, Lonnie, and Petey. In addition to preserving their meal, bedtime, and outings rituals, Peter involved the children more in meal preparation, during which time he would spend time talking with whichever child was helping. Family prayers also became even more meaningful, now as a time to communicate with and about Cindy. They continued to do their annual camping trip with their former church in Connecticut, and now they added regular visits to the cemetery to connect as a family around their memories of Cindy. When the first Christmas came after Cindy's death, they headed for California to create a new way to ritualize the holidays, rather than stay at home and dwell on their losses.

For postdivorce families, certain rituals of celebration can be occasions for demonstrating that the original family can still pull together. Joe came to his daughter Georgia's birthday parties for several years after his separation and divorce. Her birthday party had always been a grand occasion for her and the extended family, since she was the oldest of all the grandchildren and her birthday fell on January 1. Joe and his ex-wife, Lucy, decided that he would be present to show family solidarity in support of Georgia on her birthday. The event also helped keep Joe connected with his former in-laws, with whom he always got along. This arrangement worked for about five years, until Lucy got remarried. The first birthday party after the remarriage was quite uncomfortable for the three adults, and Georgia could feel the tension. Joe then decided to end his participation in the extended family birthday party and to have his own birthday party for Georgia on another day.

This story exemplifies how flexible postdivorce families must be if they want to be intentional about their rituals. It was helpful and constructive for Joe to appear at his daughter's parties in the early years after the separation, just as it is for some parents to go to school conferences together. This level of participation works when the ex-spouses are genuinely cooperative as fellow parents and can put the child's interests first. Some ex-spouses come together for Christmas Eve gift opening the first year after their separation, particularly if the divorce is not yet finalized. But they must be aware of what this means, and does not mean, and be clear to the children that being together for a family celebration does not mean that they are getting back together.

Over time, however, most families of divorce find that they need to create separate celebration rituals, as their separate families and households form their own boundaries.

When a friend of Barbara's became a single mom, she knew that she would have to do Christmas in a new way. Many family rituals had been built, but things were different now. She said a little prayer and approached her three children with the idea of spending Christmas morning serving a meal at a shelter. It meant that they would have to get up very early to drive to the nearest large city. They would spend the morning cooking, setting tables, and then serving and sharing the meal at noon. There was disbelief and grumbling. These children were used to piles of presents and an affluent holiday. But bright and early they all appeared, dressed and ready for their new adventure. It has become their ritual now for six years and it has brought a deeper new meaning to the whole idea of Christmas.

Even then, coming together for major occasions such as weddings, graduations, and bar and bat mitzvahs may be important demonstrations of united support from the child's two families.

For the nonresidential parent, it is also crucial to hold on to old rituals that still work, to modify others, and to create some from scratch. The biggest mistake nonresidential fathers make is to have free-form, unstructured weekends that flit from one distracting activity to another. The father eventually runs out of fun things to do with the children, and the children become worn out and demanding. And little parent-child connection occurs. Creating a family atmosphere means having both family rituals and time to hang around rather than trying to be a camp activity director or Disney Dad. Nonresidential parents can develop rituals that become special to them and their children. One father, an avid swimmer, took his children swimming every time they visited, and coached them on their swimming techniques, a form of recreation and attention that was special to Dad and his kids.

Thanksgiving, Christmas, Passover, and other important family-focused holidays are often treacherous times for single-parent families. Because being alone without one's children at these times can be terribly lonely and depressing, it is not surprising that some ex-spouses compete for their children. There is no better way to ruin the ritual for the children than for them to feel they are hurting one of their parents by being with the other. When both parents are still involved with the children, most families develop fixed holiday schedules in order to balance everyone's needs. In the case of the DiAngelo family, the children alternated Thanksgiving each year with each parent. For Christmas, they split Christmas Eve and Christmas Day between households, with the sequence of houses alternating each year.

It is crucial that the scheduling of major holiday and religious rituals be routinized in single-parent families, rather than fought over each year. This requires that both parents support the arrangement and manage their own sadness and regret without drawing the children toward their own side.

Strategies Used by Single-Parent Mothers

We asked single-parent mothers what they have done to make family time special, and here are some of the strategies and tips they shared, in their own words:

• I do special things with one child at a time, something that each child enjoys doing alone with me.
• I recognize each child's birthday once a month. (If they were born on September 19, then we celebrate on the nineteenth of

each month.) It might be something as small as getting a haircut, but it is their special time.

• Sunday is kids' day. I do whatever they want.

• When I need to know something from my daughters, I ask them to join me on a walk. By the end of the walk, they open up completely.

• With shared custody, every holiday is different, nothing regular. But I try to teach the kids that the important thing is that we are together, not the date on the calendar.

• People think I'm nuts, but I invite their dad for birthdays.

• We make a big deal of breakfast. I play music that I want them to hear, make a lovely breakfast, spend time talking.

• I go to their rooms in the evening, listen to their music with them, and give them a back rub. Then they want to talk.

Are you as impressed by this list of activities and strategies as we are? Behind each story is the mind and heart of a thoughtful and determined, yet often exhausted, parent. We are struck that most of these activities do not take a great deal of additional time out of a parent's day—minutes for the most part. It's the mindfulness and the persistence that count more than the sheer amount of time. It's the small things that tell children, over and over until it's imprinted in their hearts, that they are safe and loved by a parent who, no matter what the burdens of raising children alone, puts family life first.

Putting Family First
in Stepfamilies

If you love me, you spend time with me. That's the elementary
logic of family life for children. It's also the basic understanding of
adults in a new marriage, although, as we have said, many couples
drift away from that expectation as daily life becomes hectic and
complicated. Can you see how a collision course is created in new
stepfamilies between the needs and expectations of the children,
the parent, and the stepparent?

Children, the first set of characters in the drama of stepfamily
life, would like to own their parents' time. Young children want
their parents within hailing distance at all times. Older children
want their parents available on demand. After a divorce, children
get less total parental time because their parents are in two different households. Then one or both parents date again, a frighten-
ing prospect for many children. As the relationship becomes more
serious, the couple spends more time alone—again, not something most children would vote for. After the wedding, the hardest phase of all begins. After years of having Mom or Dad's full
attention at home, the children now must share it with the new

mate. Even if the couple have already lived in the same household with the children, generally something important changes when they become a married couple.

Enter the second major character in the drama—the new spouse, now also known as a stepparent. ("Step" comes from the Old English word for "bereaved.") This person generally focuses first on establishing a new marriage, and secondarily a new family. (For the most part, the new spouse would gladly have gotten married without any stepchildren being present.) Since the marriage comes first, the new spouse desires time alone with the partner, and for rituals of connection and intimacy. After all, the courtship involved lots of couple time and couple rituals. The new spouse/ stepparent may think, perhaps naively, that being together in the same household will lead to even more time to connect.

Enter the third character—the original parent. (We use this term rather than "biological parent" because some are adoptive parents.) Here we have two agendas—lots of time with the new spouse and lots of time with the children. In the classic triangle, we have the children and the new spouse each wanting from the original parent a good deal of the scarcest commodity in contemporary family life—time. Many original parents say they feel pulled—even pulled apart—by the demands of their children and their spouse.

These naturally competing needs turn time into an almost politicized issue in some stepfamilies. Mary Ann always had a glass of warm milk with her daughter Erin at 10 P.M., when they would talk about the day. Guess where Mary Ann was at 10 P.M. after her new husband, Steve, moved in? Erin started to act out, for reasons that were mysterious to her mother. The mistake was not that Mary Ann prioritized time with her husband at bedtime, but that she did not replace this lovely ritual with her daughter.

Steve, for his part, loved to travel. He pressed Mary Ann to travel around the country and especially overseas a couple of times a year. The teenagers were old enough, he pointed out, and their father should be willing to house them for a week or two at a time. Mary Ann, sensing that the new stepfamily was fragile, was reluctant to leave the children during the first year of the marriage. And she was sympathetic to their desire not to spend that much time with their father, who had been only sporadically involved with his daughters over the years and who was continually behind in his child-support payments. Mary Ann and Steve did go to Italy during the second year of the marriage, and things worked out okay, but Mary Ann was not eager to try it again, while Steve saw the success of this vacation as evidence that they should travel regularly.

All of these complications would be present even without today's scheduled hyperactivity in family life. Like many parents, Janet has enrolled her children in a wealth of enrichment activities that were a burden to maintain while she was a single parent. Now that Keith, a good-natured man, has married into the family, Janet welcomed an extra chauffeur and sidelines cheerleader. Keith, who had no children of his own, did not know what he was in for. It's one thing to gulp down dinner in the car three days a week so that you can get your own child to practices and games, but it's quite another thing to do so for a stepchild whom you are just getting to know, who complains when you are five minutes late, and who never thanks you for your trouble. On top of that, you feel as if you never see your new wife except at bedtime, when you are both exhausted.

Without a perspective on how natural and common these time binds are in stepfamily life, mostly the adults and children do what comes naturally: they complain and criticize. The stepparent complains about being used and neglected, and criticizes the spouse's parenting and the children's selfish, entitled behavior. The original parent complains about being torn apart by impossible demands, and criticizes the spouse for being selfish and mean to the children. The children do their part by complaining that their life is not what it was before and criticizing their parent for neglecting them and their stepparent for being strange and mean. We may be exaggerating here, but the elements of the scenario will sound familiar to many people in stepfamilies, especially during the early years.

How can stepfamilies avoid the worst of this time bind and get out of it when it has occurred? The simple answer is that *stepfamilies must work even harder to make family life the top priority than other kinds of families, because there is less glue to start with.* An original two-parent family that gets into a hyperactive state can draw on years of bonding. It has gas in the tank. A single parent can draw on the intense connection of the years of being solo with the children, day in and day out. But a new stepfamily is a family in formation, not yet a well-bonded unit. It often takes five years or more for everyone to feel secure that the time and attention paid to one member does not detract from a relationship with another, and for patterns of authority and discipline to be worked out. Dawn and Tom had several strategies for combining their two families. In Dawn's words:

> Through the years as a blended family we have reclaimed lost family time often by removing the TVs from our living areas and storing them for a few months. This tactic, although not popular with my children when implemented, fostered family communication, reading, and playtime while also creating an environment conducive to successful homework completion and instrument practice.

During this extended adjustment period, all stepfamilies have to be above average in staying away from overscheduling and being isolated by electronic media, so that they can finesse their family time and family rituals. When you set the new glue in place, you've got to hold steady for a while to let it set.

Finessing Rituals in Stepfamily Life

As challenging as they can be, single-parent families don't hold a candle to stepfamilies when it comes to complications of family rituals. In single-parent families, there generally is one ritual tradition to draw on from the previous two-parent family. And in each household, there is one adult making decisions about family time. In remarried families that follow divorce, there are several sets of ritual traditions to contend with—the original family's plus one or two stepparents'—and two adults making decisions in each household. People approaching a second marriage often don't realize that they are not just uniting as a couple, but are merging at least two family cultures.

The preparation for a remarried family begins during the courtship of the couple. Here the couple are establishing their own rituals of connection by spending long blocks of time alone getting to know and enjoy each other. They must decide on the timing of involving the new partner with the whole family's rituals. Bev's children didn't meet Mark until they had dated for six months and they knew that they were serious about this relationship. It was another year before they married. During that time Mark came over for dinner and the family went boating or biking. Bev remembers these as fun activities that made it easy for them all to interact and get to know each other.

If the children feel that the new romantic partner in Mom's or Dad's life is brought into core family rituals too soon, before there is a clearly committed relationship, they might reject that person at the outset. Examples are a child's birthday party or at the family

Christmas gift opening. Such intimate participation in the family's ritual life should probably be postponed until the relationship is serious and there has already been a good deal of bonding with the children.

Planning for the remarriage ritual itself is pivotal in the formation of a remarried family. Janine describes how she and her future husband decided to have a yearlong engagement in order to emotionally prepare everyone, including themselves, their children, their parents, their siblings, and even their ex-spouses, for the coming marriage. One advantage of a remarriage is that you get to shape the ceremony pretty much the way you want, as opposed to a first marriage where other people are likely to have definite expectations about what should happen at the wedding. A disadvantage is that some of the participants will have mixed feelings about being present. Children in particular may see the remarriage of one of their parents as a sign that their parents will never get back together, a hope the children may have harbored. Extended family members and friends will have their own feelings about the breakup of the first marriage, about who was mostly responsible for it, and about the likely success of the second one. Even though not invited, ex-spouses, living or dead, are also a real presence at the remarriage ceremony in the minds of nearly everyone. The ghost of marriage past hovers over the ceremony.

Bev and Mark were very deliberate in how they involved all the children in the wedding. One son walked Bev down the aisle, her daughter carried a bouquet, and her youngest son rang the church bell. In another family, when the groom put the wedding ring on his new wife's hand, he turned around and put a locket around his new stepdaughter's neck. In a family that involved older children, some grown, the new couple gave each other's children their own special friendship box to symbolize their intent to be a friend, not a replacement parent.

Everyday rituals and rituals of celebration can be tricky in the early years of remarried families, especially if there are children present from both sides. George brought into the remarriage a quiet seven-year-old daughter who lived with him part-time. Their dinner meal ritual had been a low-key father-daughter conversation, often with long periods of silence since neither was very talkative. Geri brought two in-your-face teenagers and a more random dinner ritual that involved loud talking, friendly arguments, and a television blaring in the background. In the midst of a conflict over dinner rituals, George used the term "barbarians" to describe Geri's children, a term that Geri never let him forget. She commented on his daughter's "lack of any personality," a criticism he never let her forget. Each was feeling accused of being a poor parent. The truth was that they were both good parents but had to learn to blend the cultures of their family rituals. In therapy, they learned to compromise and create daily rituals they could live with. In the case of dinner, the television went off but there was no censoring of the level and tone of the conversation, although Geri did agree to avoid bringing up disciplinary matters during the meal.

Sometimes children signal their negative feelings about the remarriage by refusing to deal with a stepparent during family rituals. Joyce's teenage daughter Carrie would not talk to her new stepfather, Peter, at dinner. After months of being ignored and feeling hurt, Peter told Joyce that he would not eat with the family anymore. This precipitated a crisis. Joyce felt helpless to make her daughter relate to her new husband, and she did not want to have either her daughter or her husband boycott family dinners. In family therapy, the couple learned that their whole meal ritual was being twisted around Carrie's silence toward Peter. Joyce would focus on Carrie in order to draw her into the family conversation, thereby making Peter feel even more left out. Their solution had two parts. Peter would work on not taking Carrie's behavior as a personal insult; he came to see himself as a convenient target for Carrie's upset about the marriage along with her general teenage woes. Joyce would keep Peter in the conversational loop and resist the temptation to pursue Carrie to get involved. Eventually, time, patience, and Carrie's growing maturity level moved family dinner rituals from awful into the acceptable range. Some remarried family rituals, especially in the early years, may not be highly satisfying, but to discard them would undermine the formation of the new family.

Stepparents can use rituals of celebration to forge bonds with their stepchildren. Birthdays in particular offer opportunities for the stepparent to offer the child a personal gift, not one bought with the other parent. George found that giving sporting equipment to Geri's teenage son, Curt, at his birthday gave them something to share during the rest of the year. In the same way, a stepparent can offer special outing rituals that the children might not have done with either of their original parents. One stepfather, an avid hiker, developed an annual camping trip ritual with his stepson. The first year, the mother was planning to go but had to pull out at the last minute because of a work commitment. Her husband and son went anyway and had a wonderful time. In subsequent years, the trip became something the stepfather did alone with his stepson. Mom wisely stayed away. In another family, the new stepmother bonded with her stepdaughter through the ritual of shopping trips accompanied by a stop for ice cream on the way home.

Dawn, the mother of three boys, talks about rituals that have developed as her boys and their stepfather engage in "guy things." One important ritual began when her husband took her oldest son to Colorado to climb the Rocky Mountains in celebration of his graduation from high school. Her other two sons are already planning their "trip with Tom" when they graduate. Tom still takes his adult daughters on separate vacations. A new ritual started with his stepsons. It developed when it was time for the boys to visit their biological father. Tom initiates a special meal honoring the boys just before they leave for their visit and greets them with a specially decorated Dairy Queen ice-cream cake upon their return. These kinds of connecting rituals can slowly build a one-to-one relationship between stepparent and stepchild.

In the midst of all these efforts to facilitate bonding between one's new spouse and the children, and between stepchildren, it is important that parents maintain rituals of connection with their own children. Some remarried parents make the mistake of trying to "blend" the new family by not paying special attention to their own children. Ross, thirty years old, still had painful memories of what happened between him and his father after his father remarried following the death of Ross's mother. For years, Ross and his father had gone to baseball games together, their core ritual of connection. The new stepmother opposed this outing because she thought that one-to-one time between her husband and his children undermined the unity of the new remarried family. Under this pressure, Ross's father abandoned the ritual. Many years later, Ross still felt abandoned by his father. The most successful remarried families encourage special rituals of connection between parents and their children.

Family vacations are often the stuff of nostalgia: the family cabin, the beach, the trip to the mountains, the visits with Grandma in the country, and so on. Figuring out what to do with two different family vacation traditions requires high levels of diplomacy and skill. Smart stepfamilies tend to discuss and negotiate vacation plans far in advance, rather than waiting until decisions have to be made. Sometimes the logistics of a full remarried family vacation are nearly impossible, especially if the children spend considerable vacation time with their nonresident parent. There might be four adult vacation schedules to juggle, plus children's sports, camp, summer school, and other activities. Even if the family can find a time to vacation together, not everyone will be pleased with the plan. However, some remarried families deliberately alternate trips that give one side of the family or the other the chance to do what they previously enjoyed doing. Letting everyone know that turns will be taken can cut down on the complaining. Other families deliberately do things that neither side had done previously. Overall, it is best not to force family vacation rituals in the early years of a new remarried family. They are better finessed, experimented with, and nurtured along until the new family finds its groove.

Nowhere do loyalties to old rituals surface more than at the holidays, at least for families who celebrate them. The holidays are defined by memories of how the rituals should be done correctly in all their details. Children tend to be conservative when it comes to holiday rituals; they like things the way they have been. The most successful remarried families form a creative amalgam of holiday rituals. They use existing rituals from each side of the family, and they grow their own new rituals. This whole delicate process is best done with open discussion rather than by parental decree. That is, the parents and children should discuss together how they would like to do such holidays as Thanksgiving, Christmas, or the High Holy Days during the first year of the remarried family. Each tradition is granted respect in the conversation; parents may have to enforce this rule if children ridicule the "crazy ideas" of the stepparent or stepsiblings. Holidays are best approached experimentally in the early years of remarried families. Assume that some rituals will work and others will not. Settling into a widely accepted pattern of holiday rituals may take five years or more, even for highly intentional remarried families.

For the Mathiasen family, distance prohibits splitting the holiday between the two parents, so they alternate Christmas. On the year when Bev and her new husband, Mark, don't have the children, they spend the holiday with another couple whose children are also gone. These two couples are building a new ritual that supports their new family structure.

As we've said, putting family first in a stepfamily may be harder than in other family units, because stepfamilies are composed of two, three, or more distinct families. Each of these subfamilies—Mom and her kids, Dad and his kids, Mom and Dad and their new kids, plus ex-spouses and kids—has its own needs for time and rituals of connection and celebration. For this reason, couples heading stepfamilies have to be especially intentional about managing family time. All stepfamilies are preceded by loss—the breakup of the relationship of the original parents through death or divorce. But they are born from a love that represents a renewal of hope in the possibility of an enduring marriage and a nurturing family for children to grow up in. Putting family life first in stepfamilies takes years; when accomplished, it is a remarkable human achievement.

The ideas for meals, bedtimes, get-aways, and so forth listed throughout the book can certainly be used by stepfamilies.

11

Making Time for a Marriage

Let's be blunt: if you are married with children, the odds are good that time for your marriage is near the bottom of your priorities. Not that your marriage itself is a low priority, or that you don't love your spouse deeply. But for most couples, time with a spouse for personal conversation, mutual fun, and sharing common interests gets crowded off the family calendar by a long list of more pressing activities. We schedule time for nearly everything these days, except our marriages.

Getting married and having children is like launching a canoe in the Mississippi River at St. Paul, Minnesota. If you don't paddle, you go south. The river current respects no one's good intentions or fondness for St. Paul. In the same way, the swift, demanding currents of parenting and work responsibilities pull the best of couples into a place where they live more like co-parents and partners in a family business than like friends, lovers, and confidants.

Of course, it doesn't have to be this way, and some couples are exceptions. But a sad irony in contemporary family life is that many people who are good at making time and space for their children are bad at doing the same for their spouse. We evolve good parent-child rituals over the years, but we lose our marital rituals. We can be gifted at rituals with the whole family—family dinners, camping trips, vacations—and dumbfounded about what we would do as a couple. Some couples who courted through long, romantic dinners are nervous about dining alone because they are not sure what they would say to each other for an hour or more. So they make sure to invite other people along for company. When it comes to long-range planning, many of us are good at planning for our children's future but don't talk about how we will be a couple when our children are older. If we are honest, how many of us would give ourselves the same grade for effort in our marriage as for effort in our parenting? How many of us would die before putting our parenting on hold for weeks but end up putting our marriage on hold for years?

So What's Wrong with Putting the Children First?

In some ways we have to put our children first. They are the most vulnerable and needy people in our homes. When you want to make love with your mate and your wet, hungry baby wakes up and starts crying, you know what you have to do. When your teenage daughter is beside herself after just being dumped by her boyfriend, you put your spouse's bad day on hold and attend to your daughter. Children also enrich our marital lives by their love, their joy, and their openness to what is new in the world. On the other hand, perhaps you and your spouse used to dine alone at 8:30 P.M. with a bottle of wine, but once you had kids you rightly established a family dinner ritual closer to 6:00 P.M., and you now drink milk along with the kids.

Adjustments like this are natural and inevitable. But there is a difference between adjusting your marriage to meet your children's needs and losing your marriage to parenthood. We think of Dave and Deirdre, loving parents and empty spouses. Somewhere between their son's birth and age six, their kids became their whole world. It began with never getting a sitter for the baby. Their excuse was that they were living away from extended family and did not trust the local babysitters. This may make sense for a newborn baby, but even then Dave and Deirdre could have looked for other responsible new parents with whom they could exchange sitting on a weekend night. But they stopped going out on dates together.

When their child was old enough to stay awake into the evening hours, and to resist going to bed, the couple never set a bedtime for him. He stayed in their midst, absorbing their attention, until he fell asleep on his own and was carted off to bed. Soon afterward, the couple went to bed themselves, drained from the day's work of earning a living and caring for a child. Then their daughter was born, and the pace of parenting quickened, absorbing even the small snippets of couple conversation they had stolen when they had just one child. Dave and Deirdre were not unhappy with their lives. They were devoted parents and cooperative companions. They thought that's what marriage was about once you became a parent. Actually, Deirdre complained sometimes to her friends that Dave did not pay enough attention to her, but her friends assured her that he was just a typical husband and that no one has much of a marriage when the children are little.

Their family life became even more child-centered when their son started playing soccer at age six. It turned out that he had talent, and his parents enjoyed watching him play. In a scenario we have discussed at length in this book, they enrolled him in a more competitive team, a traveling team that practiced three times a week (four times during school breaks), plus home or away games every weekend. Tournaments were extra. The frequent practices meant that now they did not have family dinners very often, and the weekend travel, combined with their day jobs, meant that most weekends were pretty frantic. When their daughter, Denise, reached soccer age, she too joined the frenetic family pace, and now Dave and Deirdre frequently found themselves on separate soccer fields watching different kids. Dinner was a sandwich eaten in separate cars. Denise was not interested in a traveling soccer team, but she did sign up for competitive dance, which, it turned out, was as time-consuming as soccer.

Dave and Deirdre have a typical middle-class family in today's world, revolving around the parents' work schedules and the children's activity schedules. Notice that there is no couple schedule. At home, nearly all of their conversations center on the children or household logistics. Dave and Deirdre love each other, and sometimes talk about worries or stresses from their work or about the failing health of his father and her mother. But these conversations, like all their couple interactions, get interrupted constantly by the children. The parents could not imagine asking their children to refrain from interrupting a couple conversation. Nor could they imagine requiring their children to get to bed at a certain hour so they could have some off-duty time to relax together. Although they do get babysitters now, their occasional evenings out are with friends or to see a movie—not to spend time in quiet, personal conversation where they might reconnect emotionally. And their sex life, as you might imagine, is pretty stale at this point. It takes more than being good parents to keep intimacy alive.

If you think Dave and Deirdre have a challenge, take a look at Marc and Liz, a remarried couple who have her kids around full-time and his every other week. Like many remarried couples,

Marc and Liz have great difficulty making their relationship a priority without alienating the children. During week one, Marc tries to get some time with Liz in the evening, but her children insist she help with their homework after they return from soccer practice. She feels torn between her husband and her children, and chooses to spend the time with her children because she believes they need her more. During week two, when Marc's kids are with them, he is a full-time parent to them, scheduling himself every evening for their events and being available to them every minute otherwise. When Liz complains that he is not a husband during these weeks, he responds that he only has his kids every other week. And all along, the children are developing a sense of entitlement to their parent's time and attention and would raise a great stink if the couple acted like they were married lovers. Marc and Liz's situation is more challenging to their marriage than Dave and Deirdre's because in remarriages a spouse's time spent separately with his or her children feels more distancing to the other spouse than in a first marriage, where the children belong to both parents equally.

We are not saying that these two couples have chosen the wrong path in life; there are many ways to be married and few of us achieve all of our initial life goals. But a couple who do not make time for their relationship put themselves at risk in today's culture of personal entitlement. At some point one of the spouses might start to think, "Is this all that life offers me? Am I really happy in this marriage? Could somebody give me more intimacy in my life?" As Bill wrote about in *Take Back Your Marriage: Sticking Together in a World That Pulls Us Apart*, many people turn a critical eye on their spouse when they start feeling twinges of sadness about the marriage that might have been. They think they should find a new canoe mate and start again at St. Paul. But the Mississippi will play no favorites with the next marriage either.

Why Do We Give Away Our Marriages to the Kids?

No engaged or newly married couple wants to have a parent-rich, marriage-poor family life. Almost everyone wants an emotionally intimate marriage along with solid co-parenting. So why do so many of us start the process of resigning from being spouses after we become parents?

For starters, children are natural and eager consumers of whatever time, attention, and services parents provide. It's the job of parents to discern how much is enough, how much is too much, and to enforce the difference. Many good parents avoid spoiling kids with material things, except for buying them electronics, which seems to have no limits. But setting limits on how much time and attention we give them, and how many opportunities and activities we provide, is not stressed in our culture. Children nowadays own their parents. In a swift turn of a generation or two, we went from the norm that children should be seen and not heard when adults are around, to the norm that it is only the children who should be seen and heard when adults are around.

Parenting, then, has become like operating a twenty-four-hour-a-day, seven-day-a-week store, with service on demand. Of course, parenting has always been a full-time job, but nowadays it's not just being on call for children's core needs, but being ready to respond instantly to their wants and whims as well at any time of day or night. When children are little, they want constant face-to-face time with you as a parent, or at least they want you in the next room and available to meet their needs, wants, and whims (which, to young children, are indistinguishable). When they become mobile teenagers, they want you to be on a twenty-four-hour cell phone leash in case they require information or permission for some activity. (But don't ask them where *they* are!) A newspaper columnist wrote about her resentment and rebellion against always having her cell phone turned on for a daughter who scolds her when it is turned off. Who, you might ask, are the parents and who are the children?

On the home scene, children of all ages now have a new universal human right to interrupt adult conversation at any time and for any reason. The adults must disengage from their conversation and turn immediately to the child. Many parents now define rudeness, not as a child interrupting willy-nilly for a minor reason that could wait, but as adults putting the child off while finishing their sentence about an illness of a family member! It would be rude to keep talking or to ask the child to say "Excuse me" and request permission to interrupt. Can you imagine telling your seven-year-old, who wants an answer now about tomorrow's swimming outing, to wait until you and your spouse finish talking about something? If you can, you are already resisting the pull of 24/7 parenting. If you can't imagine it but would like to, you are on your way.

One way to reclaim time for your marriage, then, is to be willing to draw a boundary at times when you are home with your children. By that we mean being willing, when appropriate, to let your children know that you are involved in a conversation or activity with your spouse that takes priority right now, and that you will attend to the child's needs in a moment. It may be as simple as a mother saying that she will help with homework in ten minutes, after finishing a conversation with the father. This signals that sometimes the marital relationship takes precedence over the nonurgent needs of the child—a healthy message to a child who otherwise can feel like a demanding customer in a store with two clerks who should not be visiting with each other and neglecting their job.

But locating spontaneous spaces for the marriage during the day is not enough. You've got to make time on a regular basis if you want to keep your marriage growing.

Couples Who Make Daily Time for Their Marriage

Some couples find ways to navigate the Mississippi without sacrificing their children or their marriage. We have to learn from them. Before they had children, Claudia and Raphael used to check in with each other by phone several times a day, and then enjoyed a leisurely dinner most nights. Once they had a baby, and then another one in short order, they found that their daytime phone chats were mostly filled with child care and household logistics—who threw up or has a cold, don't forget the milk on the way home. Dinners with babies and toddlers were not prime opportunities for personal connection. Claudia and Raphael knew they had to do something to stay in touch with each other. So they settled on the half hour before bedtime every night, when they would have a cup of herbal tea and catch up with each other. They now do this "talk ritual" religiously, tired or not, around ten o'clock every night. This is their time as a couple in a schedule otherwise dominated by jobs and very young children.

Jennifer (married forty years) likes to tell about how she and her husband survived when their three children were in their busy and demanding school-age years. Jennifer's husband, Joe, was an army officer who, when not on maneuvers, was able to be home at 5:30 P.M. every night. Jennifer made sure the children had a snack when they got home from school. Then when Joe came home, the parents had "Officers' Club." They had a drink and a conversation together in the living room for exactly thirty minutes, during which time the children were expected to entertain themselves— and stay out of the living room! Jennifer recounts how sometimes the children would gather just outside the living room carpet, waiting for the six o'clock chime to sound the end of Officers' Club and the beginning of family time. Jennifer's now-grown children tease their parents fondly about Officers' Club, but Jennifer notes that none of her children has found another way to carve out time for their spouses.

Not every couple would want to imitate Jennifer and Joe's military way, but there are other methods for creating couple time. Pete and Kathleen have a ritual. When Kathleen arrives home from work around 8:30 P.M. on weekday nights, Pete greets her and then starts the tea water. Kathleen says hi to their sixteen-year-old daughter (who is usually doing her own thing), gets changed, and then joins Pete in the kitchen at around the time the water is boiling. They sit together and get caught up with their days' activities for fifteen or twenty minutes, until they are finished with their tea.

Bill and his wife, Leah, developed a new talk ritual when they moved to Minnesota in 1986. As you know, it gets cold in Minnesota, so they bought a hot tub and put it outdoors under the stars. Their nightly ritual is that around 10 P.M., they get into the hot tub. They sit out there, look at the stars, and talk. No kids, no television, no phones, no Internet—just relaxing together to end the day. They do it every night of the year except when they have been out late or the weather makes it impossible—say, when it's raining and lightning outside or the temperature dips below –10 degrees!

These are examples of daily rituals of connection. If we could wave a magic wand, we would want every couple in the land to have at least fifteen to twenty minutes a day, without distractions, to talk as friends. If this sounds impossible, ask yourself what you wanted from marriage before you got married; would fifteen to twenty minutes a day have seemed unreasonable? No doubt it would have seemed absurd, not nearly enough!

Keep in mind some ground rules to make these daily connection rituals successful. First, once you find a time that works, stay committed to it; otherwise, you will lose it to the distractions of everyday life. If one of you is more committed than the other, the ritual will fail, because the more interested partner will feel bad about dragging the other one along. Second, pick a time that is tied to some other event, such as breakfast, an after-dinner walk, or a before-bedtime cup of tea. Third, when you are talking together, focus on checking in with each other—thoughts, feelings, worries, joys—rather than focusing on household logistics such as kids' schedules or decisions such as when to paint the house. And third, avoid getting into conflict. Almost anything negative on your mind can wait until later. If you get into too many arguments during connection rituals, you will start to avoid them. Marital rituals should be safe zones.

Couples Who Date

In addition to daily time to talk and connect, the other important ritual for keeping a marriage fresh while raising children is to continue to date. What do we mean by dating? For starters, here is what marital dating is not: it is not going to a movie, sitting in the darkened theater, and then driving home. That's seeing a movie together, not going out on a date; you might as well have watched it at home on the VCR. It is not going to dinner with another couple; that's socializing with friends, not dating each other. It is not jogging together when you enjoy each other's company but are too winded to talk; that's a good recreational ritual, not a date. Do you get the picture? Dating is going out together, just the two of you, to connect emotionally through conversation and pleasurable activities.

Barbara and her husband, Sam, knew that they would lose their marriage to the demands of four children and Sam's medical practice if they did not make their marriage a priority. One of their solutions was to book regular dates into the schedule. When the children were young and the family had little money, Barbara and Sam traded babysitting regularly with family members who had children of the same age. Later, Barbara and Sam booked Jodi Lynn, a trusted neighbor girl who came faithfully every Wednesday night to be with the Carlson kids so that their parents could rejuvenate their personal relationship. Sometimes the weekly dates came up fast and Barbara and Sam weren't sure what they were going to do, but they always found some way to turn their dates into something that kept them glued to their relationship.

Here is another couple's successful date ritual, as described by the wife. She and her husband have been married for fourteen years:

> Since the time we were married, we have taken payday as a day to go out and be together. We may only have enough money to attend the dollar theater, or even only enough money to take peanut butter sandwiches to the park. But we set aside time at least every two weeks to go out together. We have a special-needs child who demands much of our time and energy. So it becomes even more important to take this time to be alone together to reconnect and just talk as two adults. Our family problems are off-limits for discussion while we are on our date, so that the time is concentrated on just us. Recently our eleven-year-old told us that married people don't date, but we had to correct her and let her know that yes, indeed, married people date and enjoy it! You may not be able to control the circumstances in your life, but you can control how you react to them. Happiness is a choice. Carpe diem—seize the day—and make the most of it!

Notice the elements of this inspiring date ritual. They always went out, even if just to a park bench. They also did something pleasurable, even if was just to eat a peanut butter sandwich or see a second-run movie. And they always talked personally, about the two of them, and not about logistics or family problems. They had a moment of freedom from talking about their parenting responsibilities. During these dates, they took back their marriage, for a time, from the burdens of daily life.

Finding Time for Your Marriage When Raising Kids

Here we pull together our take-home messages about prioritizing your marriage while raising children.

• *Plan marital time.* Schedule your spouse. Put it on the family calendar. Write it in your personal schedule book. Enter it into your Palm Pilot. This is the chief way to paddle the canoe. One business executive, when he finally "got it" about prioritizing time for his marriage, entered "Thursday noon lunch with Monica" into his perpetual schedule. Another couple books their anniversary weekend trip for next year as soon as they finish celebrating this year's anniversary.

• *Remind yourself repeatedly that your marriage is the foundation of your family and the cornerstone of your children's security.* It is primary, not secondary, for everybody's well-being. This is not to say that children cannot prosper in a single-parent family (many do), but that in a married, two-parent family the foundation of the family is the marriage. When it goes sour, the family goes sour. A lot of research on two-parent families shows that good marriages lead to good parenting and that bad marriages lead to bad parenting.

• *Remind yourself repeatedly that your children are apt to be better fighters for their needs*—nature has programmed them to be good at getting our attention—than you and your mate are at fighting for the needs of your marriage. You've got to tilt toward your marriage in order to have balance between your marriage and your children.

• *Limit your family's outside activities* so that you have two rare elements for today's families: time to hang out as a family and time to hang out as a couple.

• *Have fixed bedtimes for your children,* after which you are off duty and can be alone as a couple.

• *Don't let your children interrupt every conversation you have with your mate.* If you really want to finish something, or if one of you needs a supportive listener, feel free to politely ask your children to come back later after you have finished talking. And teach them to ask if they can interrupt when they see you talking to your spouse.

• *Remove yourself for some important couple conversations.* Tell your children that you are going to your bedroom to talk and that you would like them not to interrupt you unless something important happens, such as someone getting hurt.

• *Carve out private space.* Consider letting your children know that your bedroom is private when your door is closed and that they should knock. This sends the message that there are certain marital times that children do not share in without checking. Consider getting a lock if your door does not have one.

• *Carve out fifteen to twenty minutes a day for a talk ritual.* Experiment until you find what works for your schedule, and then stick with it. When you find yourself drifting away from the ritual, work to reclaim it. As with starting new habits like exercise, it takes a good month or more of regular talk time to make it a lasting ritual. Watch out that you resume the ritual after you return from traveling or vacation.

• *Get sitters and go out on regular dates.* This is not only good for your relationship, but it also sends your children the message that indeed you are a couple who do special things together: you dress up, look great, and go out for a good time together. Even if they protest, even young children can handle a few hours of separation from their parents. Older children may be glad to be rid of you if they have good babysitters (our children used to suggest we go out so they could see their favorite babysitter), and they will feel more secure because they sense that you enjoy each other's company. Adolescents will be impressed that old-timers like you still date.

• *Get away for an occasional weekend together without the children.* This is a way to revive your marriage. This will depend, of course, on the ages of your children and your financial situation.

• *Make your anniversary a big deal.* Get away if you can, even for an overnight.

We teach our children about marriage by how we live our marriage. If we become full-time parental service providers, devoting little time to our marriage, our children will tend to approach their own marriages in the same way when they become parents. If you are working on your marriage, and giving time to it, be open with your children about what you are doing and why you are doing it. You don't have to give lectures, but make sure your children know that you sometimes set limits on your attention and availability to them because you love each other and want to make sure you stay close. Your explanations, of course, will be different for children at different levels of development, but children past the toddler stage can understand that you are fond of each other and like to be alone and do things together sometimes. With adolescents, look for moments when you can quietly share your philosophy of marriage as a relationship that requires time and attention.

We'd like to end with the words that Bill used in *Take Back Your Marriage* to describe his experience of making marriage a priority while raising his children.

> I don't hold out my own marriage as a model for all couples. And I don't mean to imply that we had no struggles with our children, or made no mistakes. We had our share of both. But I know we did one thing well: we taught our children that we valued our marriage without devaluing them, that more for us meant more for them, that we were mates before we were parents, and that in the solar system of our family, our marriage was the sun and the children the planets, rather than the other way around.

12

It's About Each of Us:
Changing Our Families

From what you've read so far, you probably have a number of ideas for how to make your family life a higher priority. In this chapter we'd like to help you reflect on how you might proceed from here. We will pull together some themes of the book and add some new strategies for change.

Begin by affirming what your family does well. Do you camp well together, although you wish you could do it more often? Play board games with laughter and good feelings? Have satisfying holiday season rituals? Do a rewarding community volunteer activity as a family? Tell bedtime stories that the kids and you look forward to? Ask yourself which family activities you most enjoy, and affirm what is good about them. The challenge is to build on them, not to think you have to create a new family from scratch.

Are You Ready to Make Changes?

A danger of reading a book like this is that you can feel so guilty that you decide you must do something, anything, to make your family better. And then whatever you try doesn't work, or even backfires. It's like seeing a younger, thinner version of yourself in an old photo, saying, "I must lose weight!" and then starting one of those three-day diets that crashes and burns at the local steakhouse. Realigning your family priorities is too important to approach impulsively because you feel bad about your current schedule.

So the first question to ask yourself is how strongly you feel about reclaiming family time and using it better. You may have heard the tale of frogs when they sit in water. If a frog jumps into scalding water, it will jump out immediately. But if a frog sits in a pot of water that slowly gets hotter, a degree at a time, it will sit there until the water is too hot and it dies. Many families today are in water that is gradually getting hotter, giving away one piece of family life at a time to good activities or the latest technology.

How hot is the water getting for your family? It's important to monitor how you feel about your family life, and ask yourself if you have reached the point of discomfort and loss. If so, then you are probably ready to consider major changes. On the other hand, if you are not feeling especially unhappy with your family schedule and your family rituals, then this might not be the time to make any major changes. Fine tuning might be enough. In that case, you might want to upgrade some of your family routines into family rituals or cut back a bit on one activity. You will then be in a better place to resist being too busy in the future.

Fine tuning is all that Bill and his wife, Leah, had to do in the mid-1980s, when the social pressures toward family busyness were much less than now. When their nine-year-old son, Eric, added basketball on top of soccer, violin, and Scouts, Bill and Leah realized that they were starting to lose too much family time. They then made a new policy: each child could do two organized activities at a time: one sport plus one other activity. In an era when community sports were seasonal, not year-round, with limited practices and game schedules, this new policy worked fine. The children had beneficial outside activities and the Doherty family continued to have lots of family time.

The advantage that Bill and his family had with their shift was that the pattern of overbusyness was not yet deep-rooted. If this pattern is deeply rooted in your family, as it is in many families nowadays, it is best that you search your heart and focus on your values before asking your family to make major changes. Like big ships, families have a lot of momentum on the open waters, and don't make sharp turns easily.

Getting Started

The first thing is to keep your eye on the prize: making family life more relaxed and enjoyable for everyone by reducing crowded schedules and creating conversational spaces not dominated by television and other media. Your family will probably like having more family time and family rituals once they get used to the change. The O'Leary family is an example. With two working parents and three busy teen and preteen girls, the family was riding the American family merry-go-round until the mother, Lisa, was diagnosed with breast cancer. As her husband, Bob, tells the story, this event made the parents take stock of what was most important in their lives, and being superinvolved in extracurricular activities was not at the top of the list. They realized that they had long ago ceased having family dinners, and so they decided to start there.

Bob reports that the change was not easy at the beginning. The girls did not understand why they had to dine as a family nearly every night. (The parents moved the dinner schedule to a different time so that everyone could be present.) They did the typical teen/preteen pout at meals. But after a few weeks, the dinners moved from unpleasant to "neutral" (Bob's term), and then over the next few months the meals became mostly positive and enjoyable for everyone. Now they are a fixture of the O'Leary family's life together, an anchor point in the daily schedule.

There are a number of important lessons in the O'Leary's story. One is *to seize opportunities for change* that come upon you, even if they come through unexpected or negative events. In this family's case, it was the mother's illness. In another family, it was the soccer-star daughter's broken ankle that got the family to circle the wagon trains for a time and experience what it had been missing. Yet another family spent a year overseas because of the father's job, a time when they had to rely on one another's company. After this year of "learning to be a family again" (their words), they reprioritized their time when they returned to the United States. A more common opportunity for making a big change is when a family moves to a different town or neighborhood; this is a choice point when a new kind of family balance might be created.

The second lesson is to *persevere,* which means that you have to be committed to the change. The O'Leary girls did their best to let their parents know that having regular dinners was inconvenient and boring. The parents resisted the temptation to cave in before the payoff. It would have been easy to say to themselves after a week or so, "Hey, this is not working for family togetherness. The girls are pouting and the conversations are stiff. Why are we putting ourselves through this?" Just as with good bedtime rituals that children will love once they adjust to having a bedtime, many other changes require fortitude in the parents. Children have a way of getting on board when we make changes based on our values about family life.

The third lesson is that the *parents have to be together.* We talked about this in the chapter on two-parent families. Lisa and

Bob made the decision together to take back their family life, starting with dinner, and they made it happen. If one of them had been a weak link, the other parent would have faced four resisters instead of three when the girls did their passive resistance at the dinner table. Both parents have to agree first on the values at stake and then on how to implement these values. If that is not the case, then spend your energy talking with your co-parent before you try to steer the family in a different direction.

Finding Time for Your Family: Add, Subtract, or Multiply

Every family is different, so there is no cookie-cutter strategy that will work for everyone. Here are overall strategies for you to consider when making changes in your own family.

If your family is overscheduled, you might begin by *subtracting one activity* or reducing the time you spend in one activity. In the Dohertys' case, described earlier, the parents decided that one sport had to go, and they let their son make the decision on which one to keep. In another family, the parents decided that the activity eating the most family time—their daughter's traveling dance program—would be dropped. Here are the options for subtracting from your schedule:

• *Drop one activity* that either consumes a lot of time or interferes with an important family activity such as dinner, bedtime, or religious services. When you discuss this with your child, make sure you stress the family reasons for doing this, in addition to any benefits for your child such as having more free time. Acknowledge the child's feelings of loss or anger, if these are present. And stress that this is not a punishment, but a rebalancing.

• *Reduce the intensity of involvement with a current activity.* One family told their twelve-year-old son that he could stay in soccer but not be on the traveling team because of the toll on the family and his own schedule. Another family told the baseball coach at the beginning of the season that their son would not practice or play on Sundays, because that was a family day, and that they understood that this might mean that he sits on the bench more often than he would otherwise.

· *Take a sabbatical from outside activities for a period of time.* We know several families who have taken long breaks during the summer. This can be a time to relax and regroup as a family, and then make decisions about priorities for the next year. Make sure, though, that you have thought through the kinds of activities you and your children will engage in during the sabbatical, so that it is not an empty experience. On the other hand, don't be the unpaid recreation director; engage the children at the outset of the sabbatical in making plans for activities to which they can contribute.

· *Eliminate television and other media from activities where you want family conversation.* You might move the television from the area where you eat, or at least make sure it is turned off before you eat. You might move a television and computer out of a child's bedroom in order to promote more family interaction. When they realized that their children were zoned out on television in their new SUV, one family decided to limit how much the children could watch television on family road trips.

The second overall strategy is adding family activities to your schedule. (You might have to do this along with subtracting activities, if currently there is no additional room in your family schedule.) Family meals are a good place to start, if you are not having many of them. You might add just one dinner a week, say, on Sunday night when there are usually no outside activities. Make it special, as we have talked about before. Or, like the O'Learys, you might bite the bullet and institute nightly dinners. You could put a family vacation on your calendar and inform the world that nothing will keep you from it this year, even if your kid reaches the Little League World Series. You might also add two or more areas of family time simultaneously, say, regular bedtime rituals and a weekly game night. The point of this second strategy is to look for what you can add positively to your family activities, whether or not you reduce your outside schedule. In some cases, it might be effective to make the time you have work better for the family by ritualizing your meals better, and then making the case for doing those activities more often by reducing the outside schedule.

The third strategy—multiplying—is the most radical. It involves making a major shift in how your family is living—lots of changes, all at once—both outside the home and inside the home. Some parents reach the point of saying, "Enough! Something drastic has to change. We must take back our family!" We certainly cannot prescribe such a change for your family. But some families reclaim their family time in just this way, by making a radical shift in priorities. It's the swiftest way to change, but you have to be highly motivated and ready to persevere with your kids and be seen as different, maybe even odd, by other parents in your community.

There are probably as many ways to take back family life as there are families. If you have one child, the task is different than if you have five. If you have a child who is a gifted and highly motivated athlete and musician, your challenge is different than if your kids don't care about these activities. If you are a working parent or a stay-at-home parent, your challenge is different. If there are no neighborhood kids to play with, your situation is different than if your block is full of playmates. If your own family had great dinner rituals, it will be easier for you to persevere in creating your own rituals than if your family dinners were filled with conflict or boredom. We offer no universal prescriptions, because every family is different.

But we have learned from a lot of parents that if you have decided you want to reclaim your family time and use it well, it will take discipline, vigilance, and long-range planning. You have to be thinking about next year's activity schedule this year. You have to weigh every potential new activity in light of its cost to family time and your child's free time. You have to say no to many good opportunities because they will interfere with the best opportunity you can give your child—a close family. We would love to hear about your experiences as you journey on this road less traveled, so we can share them with others. You can e-mail us at puttingfamilyfirst2002@yahoo.com.

13

It's About All of Us: Changing Our Communities

We humans are pack animals, social creatures if you will. We are more like lions who live in groups than tigers who roam alone. We raise our young in packs we call neighborhoods, schools, and communities. These in turn are embedded in larger cultures we have created. The upshot is that it is hard for us as individual parents to take back our families when the social world around us pulls in the opposite direction.

If you doubt this influence, look around most neighborhoods these days. Even on weekends and summer evenings when most parents are not working, there are few children outside playing. Not many more children are available if you call for a special play date for your child. So if you scale back your children's schedules, the odds are that there is nobody to play with in your neighborhood. To find playmates for your children, you have to hand your family schedule over to structured activities.

Do you want to keep your kids out of preschool gymnastics? Like one single mother we know, you might be told by relatives and friends that you are depriving your four-year-old of a chance to succeed, that she is already "behind." Do you think that age eleven is soon enough for competitive soccer? Your child at that point will be so far behind in skills as to be embarrassed on the field. If you have a daughter who is the cornerstone of her softball team but you want to keep Sundays for the family, the pressure will be there to share her with the community team. Does your son have a good singing voice? The choir director at church or synagogue will not be very understanding of your decision not to add this enriching and uplifting activity to the schedule. The truth is that today there is social pressure to do more and devote more time and energy to anything other than family time and personal down time.

The same pressures fall on adult leaders of school and community activities. One youth minister confessed to us that his evaluations at the end of the year are based not only on how much time a young person spent with family, but on how often the minister was able to get that young person out of the home and into a church activity. The scheduling director of a local YMCA told us that the complaints he gets from parents are never about intrusive schedules but about why the pool is not open until 11 P.M. on Sunday nights for kids who want to get in extra training laps.

Ironically, time spent in varsity sports in high school is easier to control because varsity teams are tightly regulated by states. The varsity football team cannot start practice until August, can only play a certain number of games, must end its season at Thanksgiving, and can only practice a certain number of hours per week. The community youth baseball league, on the other hand, is limited only by the endurance and ambition of the coaches and parents. One coach told us that his team of eleven-year-old boys once played eight games in seven days. He and his son didn't see the rest of the family that week. He pointed out that professional athletes have unions that prohibit such schedules!

This coach is typical of what is happening in our communities these days. He agreed to coach because his son was involved in the team and no one else was willing to give the time. He saw coaching as a way to be with his son and serve his community. He must follow a schedule that the league sets. The league leaders are the most enthusiastic parents—let's be honest, mostly fathers. These unpaid volunteers want kids to learn and succeed, and they are looking over their shoulders at the pace and intensity of the sports programs in neighboring communities. Younger kids' teams become scouting opportunities for recruitment to the traveling teams that represent the community. Without anyone's conscious decision, young children now play in the equivalent of professional farm teams, feeders for more advanced levels of competition.

It's all part of the same picture in academics, as homework is ratcheted up in today's schools, particularly suburban and elite private schools. With increased pressure for school performance, and fearful of the incursion of extracurricular activities on academics, teachers have increased their homework expectations, often as a response to parental demands. Children and families get squeezed further in the evenings, fearful that skirting either academic or extracurricular expectations will hamper college opportunities. For ambitious kids and families, most waking hours not spent in school are devoted to homework or extracurricular activities. Anything left over? Why not spend it zoned out watching television or on the Internet?

Tired from just reading this? Bill's wife, Leah, who is a pediatric nurse, tells of children in the office quietly asking to be set free from toxic schedules, often to deaf ears of parents who want the best for their kids but think that these complaints are a form of slacking off. But parents too feel the pressure. One therapist tells of droopy-eyed parents asking, "What ever happened to time to hang out?"

It's not only teachers who fight back by adding work to children's lives. Clergy and lay religious leaders feel that their activity programs are losing ground to community sports. So they clamp down on their expectations. Miss more than one confirmation class and your child will not be confirmed. Choose between being confirmed or playing in the basketball league championships. One father told us about his family's decision (which his daughter concurred with) that she would miss two tournament soccer games in order to attend her confirmation preparation weekend for her Lutheran church. The coach sent this thirteen-year-old girl an angry letter accusing her of lack of commitment. The girl was crushed and would not return to the team. The father called the coach to tell him that the parents did believe in commitment, but also in balance. The coach replied, "I don't believe in balance."

You would have thought that this father would have closed the door on his daughter's future involvement with this coach—enough of this nonsense! But sadly, he and his wife left the decision to their daughter, who, after a couple of weeks of missing the team, and with pressure from her peers, decided to go back. The father had initially agreed to let us print the coach's letter (names removed, of course), but changed his mind after his daughter decided to return to this coach's tutelage. Children want badly to fit in, and we are sometimes afraid to limit how much they must bend to make that happen.

Even this coach, though way out of line, is a reflection of broader cultural forces that have invaded childhood, family life, and communities. Ours is an age of unprecedented time pressures and fierce global competition. Technology is a chief culprit in feeding the time pressures we now experience. We expect instant communication and 24/7 availability. Family therapist Peter Fraenkel writes about the day he awakened to this reality. After noting on the New York subway the preponderance of ads for fast, fast, fast computers, Internet access lines, and on-line services, he realized that the underlying message was that his own life was "unspeakably slow." He writes in the *Psychotherapy Networker:*

> Later, when I turned the corner to my office, I noticed the same sorts of ads on several phone booths. The most aggressive, touting high-speed Internet access, was done up entirely in devilish red and said in foot-high capital letters: "THOU SHALT NOT COMMIT DAWDLING." In smaller type it explained: "Waiting for data is a sin."

Feel sinful? The problem, of course, is that the psychological development of infants, children, and youth in families is based on needs that have evolved over millennia of history and is not readily adaptable to today's high-speed Internet era. Children need security, predictability, and intense attention. (With that base, they can then handle a highly stimulating environment.) But these slowed-down needs of our children and families are out of sync with the fast-forward culture. That's why raising children well is now a countercultural act. It will take a social revolution of a generation of parents to slow down childhood and take back family life.

Beyond time pressures, the economic race has almost always been won by the swift, but nowadays you can't fall behind for even a short period of time. Job security is down, along with loyalty to employers. Individualism is up, neighborhood involvement is down, and civic engagement for the common good is way down. As author David Brock has pointed out, in previous generations wealth or an established family name could ensure success for one's children in their early adulthood—the right college, a good first job. In the current environment, even these parents know that their children must compete for everything they get, with no guarantees.

Children have always competed for grades, a place on teams, a part in the school play. But now the competition starts when they are toddlers and intensifies each year thereafter. Fear that one's child will be left behind or miss out is the parental anxiety of our age. That is why the parents who come forward to lead our children in competition become community leaders. But they are really misguided pied pipers, playing the tune of an over-the-top culture that is robbing our kids of their childhood and our families of their emotional sustenance.

We Need New Leaders of the Pack

We are saying that today's leaders of the pack are parents who, with good intentions, overschedule outside activities and underschedule family time. They boast about how busy their families are and how well their children compete. (Have you read holiday season letters recently?) They proclaim that their four-year-olds not only know their alphabet and their colors, but are fluent in French, giving them a leg up on college. They rarely talk about playing family games at home, about how close their children are to their grandparents, or about leisurely family brunches on the weekend. They push local programs and facilities to offer more opportunities, to win more often, and to schedule more intensely. And they are willing to run these activities if necessary.

There are no villains in this picture. The rest of us, influenced by the same culture, have chosen to follow these parent leaders. They are good people trying to do the best for their children in today's turbo-charged, competitive culture. They are leaders of the pack only because the rest of us have abdicated to them. It's time, for the sake of our children and families, for a change in leadership in our communities.

Putting Family First: A Parents' Initiative

To start this cultural and community change, we are among the founders of a grass-roots parent movement in Wayzata, Minnesota, called Putting Family First, which aims to build a community where family life is an honored and celebrated priority. The democratic theory underlying this work is that the families can only be a seedbed for current and future citizens if they achieve a balance between internal bonds and external activities. We believe that this balance is gravely out of whack for many families across our nation, and that retrieving family life requires a public, grass-roots movement generated and sustained by families themselves. Putting Family First is trying to influence the cultural conversation about the balance between family life and outside activities, and to create connections among parents to support one another in making personal changes.

The parents in Putting Family First believe that change must occur simultaneously in communities and in individual families. Putting Family First does not offer specific prescriptions for families, but emphasizes the importance of families making conscious choices about their priorities. Nor is the focus on sheer time spent at home, but more on how families use that time. We envision families turning their dinners into rituals of connection, playing games and recreating together, worshiping together if they are religious, and engaging in citizenship activities that build and serve their communities. Families have much to teach one another about the creative use of time, including ways to set limits on television, the Internet, and other electronic media that have the potential to dominate family life in the home.

Putting Family First believes that school and community activities contribute to a rich childhood. We do not call for any family to close its doors to the outside world. The challenge is to find a balance, which will be different for each family, between external and internal activities. We particularly value intergenerational activities that families can participate in together, such as common learning activities and ways to serve and build community. That said, most families will have to lean in the direction of internal family time in a world that pulls family members in different directions.

Putting Family First envisions a future in which organizations and groups in the community

- provide families with resources to develop deeper bonds in a fragmenting world
- offer regular intergenerational activities, so that whole families can participate
- have explicit working policies that acknowledge, support, and respect families' decisions to make family time a priority
- have explicit working policies that respect employees' efforts to create balance between work and family.

Within this vision of strong, balanced families flourishing in a vibrant democratic community, Putting Family First has created a Putting Family First Seal to reorient the relationship between families and the groups that schedule outside activities of family members. These groups include sports, religious, and fine arts programs, and other activities. The Seal (akin to the Good Housekeeping Seal of Approval) is awarded to groups and organizations with a demonstrated commitment to supporting family life while providing enriching opportunities for individuals. Here are the six criteria that organizations must meet to obtain the Putting Family First Seal:

• *Balanced priorities.* A written statement affirms that other life priorities, particularly family relationships, come first in participants' lives.

- *Clear expectations.* All time and financial expectations for participants and families are made clear in advance and in writing.
- *Family-friendly scheduling.* Scheduling is done with families' needs and schedules in mind. Whenever possible, events are scheduled so as to not interfere with family dinners, holidays, and religious participation.
- *Family decisions honored.* In written policy and in practice, decisions by participants and families to prioritize family activities are fully accepted, with no penalties or recriminations.
- *Religious commitments honored.* Children and youth are not arbitrarily denied participation in an activity if their family limits their involvement because of religious commitments.
- *Parents have a voice.* Parents have the opportunity to give feedback to program leaders about scheduling, to evaluate how well the program's values about family life are being enacted, and to make recommendations for future years.

We also believe that families have responsibilities to the organizations they sign their children up for. Here are Putting Family First's expectations for families:

- Families must make their own decisions, based on their values and priorities, about balancing family time and outside activities.
- Families must inform activity leaders in advance about limits they will place on their child's participation.
- Families have to speak up when asked to make time commitments they believe to be unreasonable.
- Once they agree to a schedule of activities, families are responsible to follow through.
- Just as activity leaders must respect family life, families must respect activity leaders and other program participants by being faithful to agreed-upon schedules.

• When a family priority requires an absence or change in schedule, the family has the obligation to inform the activity leader as far in advance as possible.

Beyond the Putting Family First Seal is parent-to-parent influence in the Wayzata community. When parents began to talk to their friends and neighbors about rebalancing their lives, their influence began to spread across neighborhoods and faith communities. Other frantic parents began to believe that they were not risking their children's future by saying no to certain activities, but rather that they were aiding their children's future. New leaders of the pack have begun to emerge. We are organizing Putting Family First Parent Groups around the community, and sponsoring Web discussion forums. If you are interested in more information about Putting Family First, including how to start one in your own community, look at our Web site: http//www.PuttingFamilyFirst.org.

Finding Willoughby

We began this book with the story of two families—a busy New Jersey family and the Peterschmidt family, who had recently made major changes in their schedule. Here is the Peterschmidts' story of how they came to make their radical shift in priorities, as told by Bugs Peterschmidt, one of the leaders in the Putting Family First movement.

> Sheets of listings from real-estate brokers in hand, my husband and I searched for the right house in the right suburb outside of Minneapolis, something for a growing family of four. We had seen parks, playgrounds, libraries, knew where the best school districts were, and had prayed hard for guidance. But no matter how many contemporary ranches on quiet cul-de-sacs I inspected, what I really wanted was a house in Willoughby.

Willoughby isn't a real place; it's something from *The Twilight Zone,* an old episode that my husband, Eric, and I had first watched years ago when we were newlyweds.

In it, a stressed-out ad executive falls asleep during his train ride home. He wakes up to find himself in an idyllic 1880s town. A band plays in the gazebo on the town square, people stroll about at a sedate pace and everyone greets one another by name. As the conductor tells him, "It's where a man can slow down to a walk, and live his life to full measure."

That's what Eric and I wanted for ourselves and our three-year-old son, Max, and for the baby that I was expecting. That, and a train room.

"A train room?" sellers inquired. Max had to explain: "A place where we can put mountains and tunnels and a train going around a town." It was a long-standing family project. We needed space to put up the model railroad Eric had had since boyhood. I wanted to keep adding to it, especially the train town. I hoped to make something fun and lasting for our kids and theirs.

Tromping through house after house, we saw a dozen cramped attics and dingy garages and playrooms where the set would never fit. Then we stopped at a two-story house that had a "For Sale by Owner" sign in the front lawn. The owner showed us the perfect basement room. "Let's take it," Eric said. The house was in good shape, the local schools were excellent, the neighbors friendly and the yard was filled with towering birches, elms and maples. I could just picture the neighborhood kids darting between the trees on warm summer evenings, playing freeze tag and hide-and-seek.

Two months later, as we unpacked our boxes, I kept gazing out the window of our new house, half-expecting an old-fashioned bicycle to roll by or to see a band play in a bandstand decorated with bunting. *Yes, this could be our Willoughby,* I thought.

We began to install Eric's train set in the basement. Our newborn, Betsy, was still in her bassinet when I laid out the streets on a huge plywood platform with the train circling town. Over the years, as we settled into our home, we added things to the set—a gazebo in the park and a white-steepled church, the spiritual center of this universe. I built factories and houses named for friends—Michelle's Chocolates for one who loves sweets, the Dodd house for another.

But it seemed like there was just never enough time in the real-life town we had moved to. What little there was seemed to fly by so fast. Before I knew it, the kids were in nursery school. I wanted to be a stay-at-home mom so I started a day-care business in our home. When Max was in kindergarten a mother I knew from the PTA called me with urgent news: "Summer T-ball sign-ups are this week." "It's only January," I said. "You need to get on the list early so you can be sure there's a place for him," she informed me. I signed up. There were swimming lessons too. I'd never learned to swim and wanted Betsy and Max to know how. Soon I was driving to the town pool two afternoons a week.

As a respite from our busy days we worked on the train set together on weekends. In the fall we drove out to the country to pick goldenrod from the side of the road. We hung it out on the clothesline to dry, then we painted it green and brown—perfect for miniature maples and elms for the streets in our train town. "We need a mountain," Max decided one day. So equipped with papier-mâché and cloth strips dipped in paste, we started crafting a craggy peak.

Elbow-deep in papier-mâché, I heard the phone ring. I dashed upstairs. The mother of one of Max's schoolmates excitedly told me about the math and science enrichment classes that were being set up. "The students don't really get enough during the regular class day," she said. "This extra time will make a big difference in high school."

High school? I thought. *Max is only nine years old.* But I signed him up. I certainly didn't want my kids to fall behind.

Our schedules became even more hectic. Max began private violin lessons in St. Paul, a 90-minute drive round-trip. And Betsy wanted to take piano. The soccer season stretched for months. The kids would rush home to do their homework, grab some muffins, and we would drive across town for 5:30 practice. Summer evenings I looked out at the empty backyard. *No wonder.* Every hour of our kids' days was filled. There simply wasn't time to play outside.

Our lives were barreling along like a runaway train. I got so tired of it one night I complained to Eric, "We're doing too much. Everything is such a rush."

"Can't we cut something out?"

"But everything is important."

Music lessons, Boy Scouts, youth group at church, my work, Eric's work. Nothing could go. And whenever the kids dropped one activity, there was always a new one to replace it. Basketball, art classes, trumpet lessons. That's what it meant to raise a child in modern-day America. I was fooling myself to think that this town—or anyplace—could be like the idealized Willoughby.

So I kept up the grueling pace until that winter, when I developed a terrible hacking cough. My lungs were so weak I panted going up our stairs. The doctor listened to me breathe, X-rayed my chest and came back with a diagnosis of pneumonia.

"I have carpool tomorrow," I moaned.

He looked at me gravely. "This is very serious. You must

have complete rest to get well. I'll give you some strong antibiotics, but your job is to rest."

For a week I slept. Day after day I lay in bed, ignoring the phone. When I finally could get up, I wandered down to the basement, turned on the light and gazed for a long time at our Willoughby. Our ideal world was only a train set. That's as close as we'd ever get. *Lord,* I asked, *what happened?*

I looked at the tracks where the train would meander past the mountain, the houses, the church, the town in which everybody knew everyone else. At a pace like that, people had time for one another. We were just in too much of a rush.

But we don't have to be. After all, we had chosen to do all these activities. I remembered an evening when a snowstorm had prevented Max from going to youth group at church. We stayed home and ate popcorn and watched videos—all of us. It was family time, the way Eric and I had once envisioned it. Why couldn't we make sure we did things like that? How could this busyness be the life God meant for us?

When I recovered from pneumonia, I set out to change things. We asked ourselves if our kids wanted to do all we had scheduled for them? As it turned out, Max was relieved to quit Boy Scouts. Betsy chose to take a break from soccer. And when someone asks me to volunteer for something at school, I don't immediately say, "Yes." Instead I say, "Let me think about it." It's not because the activities aren't worthy. It's just to allow more time for our family. That's where children pick up the values they will keep the rest of their lives. A sense of fair play, respect and fun.

On a warm spring evening not long ago, the four of us gathered in the backyard around a small blaze in the fire pit. I brought out some marshmallows and we roasted them on sticks we'd cut in the woods. Soon some of the neighborhood kids came by to see what we were up to.

"Whatcha doing?" one boy asked.

"Making smores," I said, putting my melted marshmallow and a piece of chocolate between two graham crackers. I really wanted to tell him, "Making Willoughby." But I knew he wouldn't understand what I meant. Instead, I just asked, "Want to join us?"

He did.

The main themes of this book are embedded in this Willoughby story. The initial dreams for a close family life with time to cuddle and enjoy one another's company. The gradual heating of the waters of busyness, fueled by enriching opportunities and the fear of not doing enough for one's child's future. The community pressure to keep doing more. The sense of helplessness about making real changes. And the decision to do something to re-create the parents' original dream of family life from the time before the children were born.

None of us actually live in Willoughby, which today seems truly out of the Twilight Zone. We are thoroughly ensconced in the twenty-first century. Not all of us have options about whether we work outside the home, or whether we live in our first choice of neighborhoods. But we are not islands. We are part of communities that either support our efforts to make putting family first, or undermine these efforts.

The stakes are high. Already the current generation of college students has only limited memories of quiet family time and leisurely play at home and around the neighborhood. A young reporter ruefully tells us that when he was growing up, his family had dinner together only on Thanksgiving and Christmas. We read about college freshmen at Princeton who use Palm Pilots to schedule time with their friends at 7:00 A.M. because they are so accustomed to an intense childhood schedule of activities that allowed little time for hanging out with friends. A weary ten-year-old tells her doctor that she wants to stay home more, and the doctor does not know how to bring this up to the parents.

It goes on. A stressed seven-year-old whispers to a neighbor parent that she wishes her mother would let her quit Scouts. A mother remarks ruefully that her family lives so much in the minivan that she should decorate it! A coach trying to bring balance to his community is dismayed when he comes upon a schedule for eleven-year-old boys who practice at 10 P.M. on Thursday nights at a facility forty-five minutes from home. Parents say they hate these schedules but don't know how to change them without depriving their children of opportunities. Everyone is afraid to be the first to cut back. A sane lifestyle looks strange in an insane world.

Enough, we say. We are calling for a widespread citizen movement of parents to reclaim their family time in a world that pulls families apart through scheduled hyperactivity and false promises of individual gain for children and parents. Putting Family First is a beginning. We call for a democratic initiative by parents to regain their leadership in raising the next generation, starting with taking back the irreplaceable resource of family time. We have created this problem together, and together we can solve it.

Acknowledgments

Our grateful thanks to all who shared their stories and inspired us: Greg Baufield, Leslie Bautista, Carol Bergenstal, Jim Brandl, Michael Brott, Gina Coburn, Wayne Dreyman, David Gaither, Jane Guffy, David Hoadley, John Holst, Pamela and Neil Infanger, Sue Kakuk, Dawn Marthaler, Marcia McCombs, Bugs Peterschmidt, Amanda Richards, Janet Swiecichowski, Carol Vannelli, and Griff Wigley.

Special thanks go to our editor, Deborah Brody, at Henry Holt and Company, and to our agent, James Levine.

Index

About the Authors

WILLIAM J. DOHERTY, Ph.D., is a professor of Family Social Science and the director of the marriage and family therapy program at the University of Minnesota and cofounder of Putting Family First. He has been named one of the ten most innovative therapists in the United States by *The Utne Reader*.

BARBARA Z. CARLSON is the cofounder of Putting Family First and the mother of four children. She has dedicated herself to families and children as a teacher, service learning coordinator, and director of an initiative to build healthy communities and healthy youth.